West Dickens Avenue

West Dickens Avenue

A Marine at Khe Sanh

John Corbett

Ballantine Books • New York

To my late mother, Dorothy Marie (Falt) Corbett,
who fought all of my wars with me.

Contents

Preface

Today is my birthday. Those of us who came for this twenty-fifth anniversary reunion commemorating our battle rode here on several charter buses from the Holiday Inn in Georgetown, where we are staying. We got off the buses at the cemetery visitors' center and walked the quiet pathways to Roosevelt Drive.

I had never been to Arlington National Cemetery before. There are graves and memorials to people I have never heard about. I never knew there was a Sir John Dill, a British field marshal in World War II. Sir John's grave is here. There are other famous people whom I have heard of but didn't realize were buried here: the late world heavyweight champion boxer Joe Louis, for instance.

We are in Cemetery Section 2, and I am with a group of Vietnam veterans. Some of them have brought their wives and children to the cemetery. We have come to Arlington to dedicate a monument to all Vietnam veterans who served at Khe Sanh. The memorial is two faceted: There is the silent bronze plaque on a red granite stone that came from a rock quarry in Wisconsin. At the new memorial is a young tree planted just behind the stone; we want it to grow here.

ix

It's a ginkgo tree, chosen because of its tenacity for holding onto life despite adverse environmental conditions. It is one of Earth's oldest living species.

The children present (sons, daughters, nieces, and nephews) will lay a multiflowered wreath at our monument at the end of the ceremony. The commandant of the United States Marine Corps, Gen. Carl E. Mundy, Jr., will give the dedication speech. The ceremony is beginning.

We gather around our memorial; it has just begun to rain. I liked rain in Vietnam; the fighting seemed to stop until the rain ended, or so it seemed. I don't mind this rain at all; it gives me a feeling of peace, albeit temporary.

I have mixed feelings this morning. I am glad to be here, because today is one more birthday I never thought I would see. I am also not happy to be here, but inwardly I know I must. I am here to honor our Khe Sanh brother soldiers who didn't leave Khe Sanh alive.

Our new bronze plaque on the Wisconsin granite stone reads:

REMEMBER
ALL WHO SERVED AND SACRIFICED
KHE SANH
1967 HILL FIGHTS 1968 SIEGE
WE ARE ETERNALLY BONDED
SEMPER FIDELIS
KHE SANH VETERANS
2 JULY 1993

General Mundy is beginning his speech. He is smart; he's wearing a raincoat. There are several umbrellas in the crowd. It is really starting to rain now. I am behind our new memorial, on a grassy knoll, seeking shelter from the rain under an old tree. I wear glasses, and to see the ceremony I am constantly wiping raindrops from my lenses. I strain to hear the general's words, but the noise of the rainfall is drowning out portions of his speech. I can hear bits and pieces: "I am honored to be here." "I am a Khe Sanh veteran." "Each of us here has our own powerful set of memories about Khe Sanh: some good, some not so good, some bad. . . ."

"BAM!" A flash of lightning and a clap of thunder. I dive for cover to the ground. Of all places, why does it have to be here? Of all times, why does it have to be now?

I hear more fragments of the general's speech: "The Marines today talk about you with the awe they once reserved for the Marines who went in with the first two assault waves at Tarawa or . . ." "Khe Sanh has become a part of the Corps' rich legacy of pride, of courage, of history . . ."

I am not embarrassed about diving for cover. I see some faint smiles in the crowd. Undoubtedly there would be laughter if we weren't here for this solemn remembrance. Khe Sanh veterans understand. We are as the stone states: eternally bonded.

The lightning strike and loud thunder have my adrenaline flowing. I am nervous and flinching; the noise and flash have put me on edge. They have put other Khe Sanh veterans in this gathering on edge, too, which also affects their wives and children. Thunder and lightning provoke flashbacks to the times we had to dive to the ground, or into it, for shelter, trying to stay out of harm's way, hoping to survive.

My thoughts are back there once again, as they have been many, many times before, triggered by loud noises such as this thunder. I will take you back there with me, to the place named on our stone, if you want me to, but I wouldn't blame you if you chose not to come.

Southeast Asia

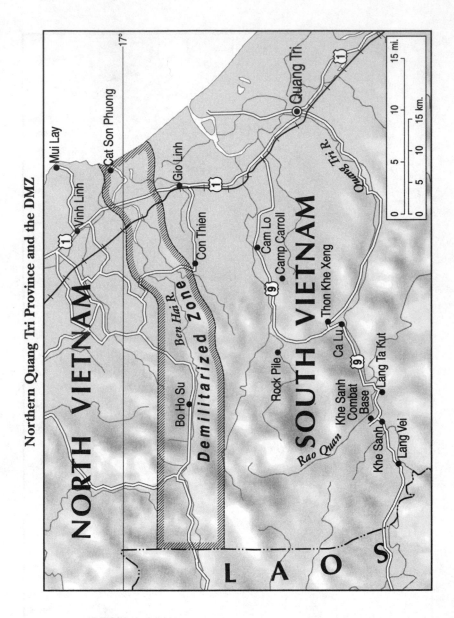

Northern Quang Tri Province and the DMZ

NORTH VIETNAM

SOUTH VIETNAM

LAOS

Mui Lay

Cat Son Phuong

Vinh Linh

Gio Linh

Con Thien

Quang Tri

17°

Ben Hai R.

Demilitarized Zone

Bo Ho Su

Cam Lo

Camp Carroll

Thon Khe Xeng

Quang Tri R.

Rock Pile

Ca Lu

Lang Ta Kut

Khe Sanh
Combat
Base

Rao Quan

Khe Sanh

Lang Vei

15 mi.

15 km.

xiv

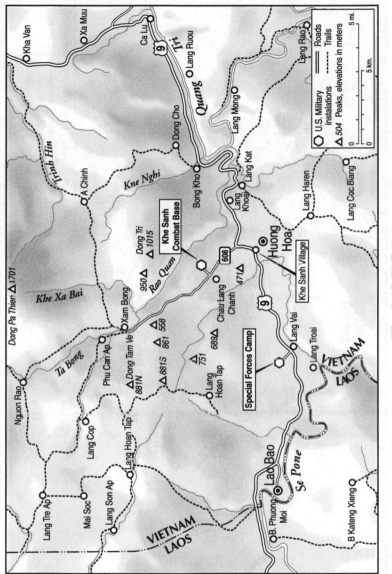

Khe Sanh Valley

The Khe Sanh Combat Base

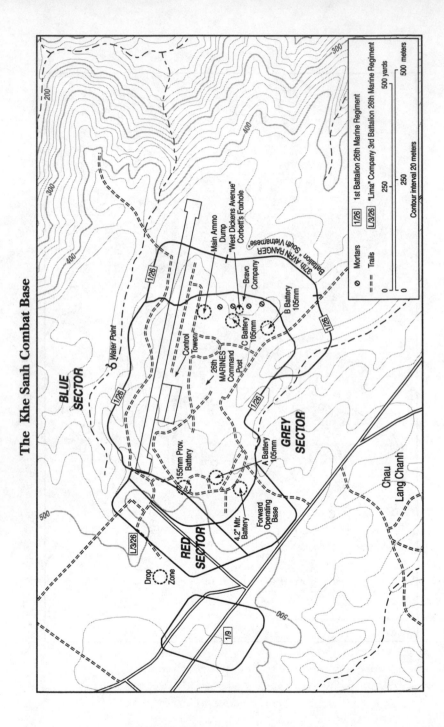

Main Ammo Dump
"West Dickens Avenue"
Corbett's Foxhole
37th ARVN RANGER Battalion, South Vietnamese

Bravo Company

B Battery 105mm

Water Point

Control Tower

26th MARINES Command Post

C Battery 105mm

BLUE SECTOR

155mm Prov. Battery

A Battery 105mm

GREY SECTOR

Forward Operating Base

4.2" Mtr. Battery

RED SECTOR

Drop Zone

Chau Lang Chanh

1/26 1st Battalion 26th Marine Regiment
L3/26 "Lima" Company 3rd Battalion 26th Marine Regiment

⊘ Mortars
= = = Trails

0   250   500 yards
0   250   500 meters

Contour interval 20 meters

1: Enlistment

Nyack, New York, July 1967

I left school during my first year of college. I romanticized about joining the French foreign legion, knowing I didn't even need to speak French. All I had to do was sign a five-year contract and they would teach me French. My youthful dreams of riding a camel across desert sand dunes, wearing a white kepi hat on my head, had faded. "Greetings," said Uncle Sam's draft notice that arrived in the mail. The United States wanted me for military service and undoubtedly would send me to Vietnam. I ripped up the draft notice in front of my mother and father at the dinner table. My act didn't go over well with my law-abiding, conservative, Irish-Catholic parents.

I decided to go to Canada and be a draft dodger. Canada is much closer than Corsica, where the foreign legion was. I wanted some adventure, but not the adventure my government wanted to provide, such as sending me to Vietnam.

I hadn't thought much about America's involvement in Vietnam. World affairs were just that, a world away, in my mind. I was rebellious and determined not to let Uncle Sam tell me what to do. I could dream about traversing sand dunes with the French foreign legion but not about being a drafted government-issue GI Joe.

1

I prepared to leave for Canada; I was going to Montreal. Even my high school French books were packed.

O'Donoghue's Tavern, 66 Main Street, Nyack, New York

The tavern was on lower Main Street, where the street slopes and terminates on the west shore of the Hudson River. The river is almost at its widest point here. The city of Tarrytown can be seen on the opposite shore, three miles across the river, night or day, except when fog enshrouds this section of the river valley. Nyack, my hometown, is twenty-five miles north of New York City. The river is not as clean as it was when Henry Hudson first discovered and explored it, sailing in his ship the *Half Moon*, but the river's towering majestic palisades haven't changed since Henry was here.

Sipping a beer, I glanced around at familiar surroundings. I wondered if I would ever see this place again. I wondered how I would do in Canada.

While pondering my future as a draft dodger, I saw a familiar face coming through the doorway of O'Donoghue's. The man walked with a limp that I didn't recall his having before. It was Tom Dunnigan, an old school chum. The last time I saw him, more than a year ago, he was leaving for Parris Island, South Carolina, the U.S. Marine Corps boot camp.

We had some beers together. He told me he had just been released from a naval hospital after months of convalescing from wounds suffered in Vietnam. His right side was partially paralyzed and he walked with a cane. He had a steel plate in his skull to close a hole inflicted by shrapnel. He was wounded in Vietnam by an enemy mortar shell. He had joined the Marines and was trained, shipped to Vietnam, and wounded, all within a year. Just months ago the parishioners at our local Catholic Church, Saint Ann's, where Tom and I were once altar boys, held a prayer service for him, because he wasn't expected to survive his wounds.

We had attended the same schools, played ball, fished, and gotten into mischief as we grew up. Conversation flowed easily that night. Over the beers I listened to his stories, one by one, about ambushes, about hills whose names were numbers on a military map, and about villages and provinces with funny-sounding names. He told me about Vietnamese people I didn't know. He said the Vietnamese had odd-sounding terms for their money: dong and piasters. I watched his eyes as he related his stories.

Tom's beers had gotten to him and he was all storied out. I was glad, because I was tired of listening to his Vietnam and Marine stories. I was ready to go home. Thoughts of Canada were still on my mind. There was a long silence at our small round table. He looked at me and stared into my eyes. Suddenly he spoke. "Jack, you don't have the balls to enlist in the Marines and go to Vietnam."

"Wanna bet, Tom?"

The Recruiter

There is courage in alcohol. I am here this morning with Tom Dunnigan at the Marine Corps recruiting station, which is nothing more than a trailer in the corner of a large parking lot at the shopping mall on Route 59 in Nanuet, a town just west of Nyack.

I am walking slowly, not because of apprehension but because Tom can't walk fast. He limps along slowly with his cane. We are an odd pair as we approach the trailer: a limping Vietnam veteran and me, sporting my 1960s-style long hair, a trademark of my rebellious generation.

This July 1967, the Marines are offering the option of enlisting for as little as two years of active duty. After two years, you are discharged. It's kind of a Vietnam War special. But there's a catch: If you enlist for only two years of active duty, you are sent to Vietnam with the infantry. A two-year enlistee receives no specialized training for a career when he becomes a civilian again. There would be no computer school, no air traffic control school, and no radar technician school. The two-year enlistee would be trained as infantry—learning about rifles, machine guns, grenades, flamethrowers, bayonets, killing—and sent to Vietnam.

I'm face-to-face with the Marine recruiter sitting at his desk inside the trailer. The recruiter has been to Vietnam and wears ribbons and medals on his chest. He forewarns me, before letting me sign the proper papers, that as a Marine in the jungles of Vietnam it will be no party. He is saying there's a good chance I will be wounded or killed. To emphasize his point, he takes a long, hard look at Tom, who is sitting next to me at the desk. The recruiter is staring at the side of Tom's head that holds the steel plate to keep his skull closed. That's the wound he got in the country where I am going. The recruiter is trying to make sure I get the message before I sign. The message I am getting is this: Though the recruiter has an obligation to recruit, he is not in the meat business. The Vietnam War is escalating as I sit here. In Vietnam, more American soldiers are dying every day.

"Where do I sign?" The recruiter shakes his head in disbelief. I don't think he wants me to enlist. I sign the papers and he half-heartedly takes them from me, one at a time. He tells me I will be hearing from him when the necessary arrangements are complete, then he suggests I get drunk, and stay drunk, until I hear from him. So I do.

Tom and I are drinking beer again, and he has a big grin on his face as he tells me that I have no idea what I've gotten myself into, enlisting in the Marine Corps. He spends the afternoon trying to prepare me.

The Following Morning

Awakening at my parent's home on Mill Street, I break the news of my enlistment. My mother is disbelieving, upset, and worried about the possibility of losing me in Vietnam. She says I should have joined the army. My dad is proud but worried. American soldiers are dying in Vietnam.

Whitehall Street

I report to Whitehall Street in New York City. The government building has worn stone steps, and as I climb them I wonder how many thousands of men before me have come up this staircase. Draftees and enlistees from adjacent counties report here to receive a physical examination. Inside, the Whitehall building is a zoo. Men crowd the hallways: conscientious objectors to the Vietnam War, divinity students who have come for a deferral, married men with children to support, and men from apple pie America who think they are doing the right thing going to this war. There are long-haired hippies wearing love beads and several men talking to themselves, feigning mental illness. Others complain of back pain, which they probably don't have.

I have passed the physical, the hearing test, the sight test, and the grab-your-nuts-and-cough test. I have left barefoot prints in the powder in a black rubber tray on the floor. The impressions show that I am not flat footed. I can walk and march.

Destination Parris Island

Our bus from New York City crosses the George Washington Bridge over the Hudson River, then carries us to Newark Airport in New Jersey. At the airport I board a propeller-driven commercial airliner that will take us to Charleston, South Carolina. This flight, my first ever, is bumpy.

It is scorching hot on the Charleston airport's tarmac. The Marines are sending a bus from Parris Island to transport us to their boot camp.

July 26, 1967, 5 P.M.

Our bus crosses the causeway to Parris Island and as we pass the sentry booth I see the guards laughing. The last sentry out shouts to us, "You'll be sorry!"

When our bus halts, four Marine drill instructors wearing "Smokey the Bear" hats board the bus screaming. They're calling us new recruits "maggots," "scummy assholes," and "puddles of puke." They grab recruits seated in the front of the bus and punch them in the stomach, then hurl them through the open bus door and onto the ground outside.

Footprints are painted on the ground outside the bus; they are painted in line and in formation, about a hundred sets. Recruits thrown off the bus and to the ground rise, one by one, and stand on the painted footprints.

I am at Marine boot camp at Parris Island. The sentry at the gate was right. I am sorry. Canada never looked so good as it does from here at Parris Island.

Platoon 3012

The number of my training platoon is 3012. The first morning in our assigned barracks, on the top floor of our brick building, four drill instructors assigned to train our platoon barge into our squad bay and attempt to put us in shock. They scream and shout at us. One asks if there are any among us who got drafted into the Marines. Like a fool, the recruit directly across from me raises his hand. The drill instructors swarm around him and scream right into his ears.

"What? You mean you didn't have the balls to enlist in our Marine Corps? You're a draftee?"

They harass him unmercifully. He can't take the pressure. He dives right through a closed window and lands with the glass shards on the concrete walk below. The drill instructors laugh. I think he's dead. For a few brief seconds I am glad I enlisted in the Marines.

In Marine boot camp I find out what exercise really means. After reveille each morning we start the day with physical training (PT) on the floor at the foot of our racks (bunks). We do so many push-ups, jumping jacks, squat thrusts, and sit-ups that each of us creates his own personal puddle of sweat on the floor. Our predawn exercise complete, we exit our squad bay and run mile after mile in the predawn darkness, jogging with flashlights so we can see and not trip on one another while running in close formation. Our drill instructor sings cadence as we run. We sing Marine chants: "If I die in a combat zone / Bag my body and send it home / Pin my medals on my chest / Tell my mom I did my best. / My granddaddy was an old Marine / Meanest man you ever seen / He ate steaks twelve inches thick / Picked his teeth with a guidon stick." There are many different chants. One chant tells about a guy named Jody who is going to steal your wife or your girlfriend while you're in Vietnam.

We take a water-survival course called "drownproofing." All the recruits jump or are pushed into an Olympic-sized swimming pool. It doesn't matter if they can't swim. The only way nonswimmers are permitted out of the water is if they go through the motions of drowning. They must sink to the bottom of the pool before the instructors will rescue and resuscitate them. Swimmers who tire and attempt to place their hand on the edge of the pool to keep afloat have their hand stomped into the pool's concrete shoulder by the boots of whichever drill instructor sees the hand first. Marine training is no party.

After close to three months at Parris Island, I graduate and continue on to advanced infantry training. I train with the Marines at Camp Lejeune and Camp Geiger, located just outside of Jacksonville, North Carolina.

I am now proficient in the use of numerous types of weapons. I have practiced with the M14, M1, M16, M60 machine gun, and Browning automatic rifle. I can disassemble, then reassemble the M14 rifle's trigger mechanism while blindfolded. I can hit a target with a rifle, without a scope, open sights, from five hundred yards away, minimum. I am proficient with a .45-caliber pistol. I have fired the flamethrower with its heavy petrol tanks strapped to my back. On the flamethrower practice range there are fifty-five-gallon drums filled with water containing soaking blankets, just in case the tanks accidentally ignite and blow up while on our back. I have fired the 3.5-inch rocket launcher, nicknamed in previous wars the bazooka. I can disarm a land mine, and I have learned to use C4 plastic explosive, which our instructor calls "silly putty" or "play dough" due to its flexibility.

The infantry weapon the Marines have chosen for me, as my specialty, is the 81mm mortar. The explosive round for this weapon is

hand dropped down its barrel. The mortar round strikes a fixed firing pin protruding at the barrel's bottom. The round is guided to
the target by math calculations transposed into degrees of deflection
(to the right or left) and elevation (up or down), and applied to the
mortar's gun sight. By leveling the bubbles in the glass vials of water
attached to the sight, the barrel is aimed at the target and made ready
to fire. I practice firing the mortar for several days. The military's nu-
merical designation of my specialty, a mortar man, is 0341.

During my training I am also exposed to tear gas. The instructors
release the gas in a chamber, then order us to take off our gas masks
and, while choking, sing the Marine Hymn. They position muscular
instructors at the exits so no one can flee until our time exposed to
the gas is officially up. When my time is up, I am back outside the gas
chamber, my skin seemingly on fire, my nose running, and I can't see.

After advanced infantry training we are given a leave home, along
with orders to report to Camp Pendleton, in California, when our
leave time is up. Marine Corps training has been tough. It has
strengthened and toned muscles I didn't know I had, and has added
inches to my chest and neck. As my training comes to an end, I am
confident that I'm as ready as I will ever be. Where is this enemy they
call the Viet Cong?

Christmas Day 1967

It is Christmas morning. I walk along the beach north of the pier in
Oceanside, California. I have used my last night's liberty and prepare
to report back to the Marine base at Camp Pendleton. If I miss the
muster, they will think I'm AWOL (absent without leave). I will be
leaving for Vietnam within a week. This isn't a very Merry Christmas.
I am looking at surfers riding the waves and wearing wet suits.

Before leaving for Vietnam, I receive my final immunization shot,
the gamma globulin. Tomorrow I will spend some time in our Quon-
set hut barracks writing letters. I will gather my personal belongings
and pack them in my seabag, then I'll stand by for further orders.

Nam Bound

It is after sunset and we are on a Flying Tiger airliner somewhere over the Pacific Ocean. The plane is under government contract. We took off from Norton Air Force Base, at San Bernardino, California.

The plane lands in Anchorage, Alaska, for refueling. We disembark for thirty minutes and find a souvenir stand, where I buy an oil lamp shaped like a dogsled; it has an Eskimo at its helm to guide the team of ceramic dogs. I will send the lamp home to my parents in Nyack as a gift.

The next stop is Okinawa. There is lots of laughter on our plane, as if we are on vacation. We have two stewardesses, but really only one. One is hiding because the Marine seated next to me shoved his Polaroid camera under her skirt and snapped a picture using a flash. Sure enough, it took sixty seconds to develop, then he passed a picture of her crotch around the plane. She fled crying into the crew quarters and we haven't seen her since. She wasn't wearing panties.

We are out of our seats and in the aisle. Someone brought along a flask of whiskey, and we pass it around. The pilot requested that we return to our seats because he is having difficulty keeping the plane at proper flying trim. We, his human cargo, unevenly dispersed about the plane, are affecting the pilot's efforts to keep the plane flying level.

Okinawa

When I disembark from the plane, I learn that the New Year just arrived here in Okinawa. We have chased the New Year flying through different time zones.

At Okinawa we receive more paperwork to take to Vietnam. I place the seabag containing my personal belongings in storage; I won't see these possessions again until I return from Vietnam, if I do.

I have put a letter in my seabag that is addressed to me and signed by me. In my letter I congratulate myself for returning safely from

Vietnam. I have put the letter just inside the seabag opening, so it will be the first item I see if I make it back to Okinawa.

Vietnam

Every seat on this flight to Da Nang is taken. This is it! We are on our way to Vietnam. There are two working stewardesses for this airplane, and no one on board is in a joking or mischievous mood. Reality has finally set in.

One stewardess is flirting and passing out her phone number, and several Marines are dumb enough to take it. What are they going to do with a phone number when they're in Vietnam? Are they going to call her from the middle of the jungle? Do they think there's a phone booth in the middle of some rice paddy? The flirting stewardess knows that she will never see any of us again, but at least her come-on puts a smile on a couple of soldiers' faces.

Then there is complete silence. Everyone, including me, retreats to his inner thoughts. We are almost there.

Final Approach

"Gentlemen, we'll be landing in Da Nang in ten minutes. It's eight A.M. local time. You're just in time for work. May God watch over you and return you all safely home. Good luck. God bless."

There is still complete silence as the plane makes course adjustments to approach Da Nang from over the South China Sea. We are landing.

2: Vietnam

The New Arrivals

The heat in Vietnam is visible. I can see it rise in waves of disturbed, rippled air from the concrete tarmac. This intense heat reminds me of walking into my mother's kitchen when the oven has been on for several hours.

We assemble in formation near the plane. Directly across from our formation is another formation of soldiers. They are Vietnam veterans who are going home on the same plane that just transported me here. We, the new arrivals, stare at them. They don't resemble us in any way, not even their clothing. They look aged and extremely tired. Their eyes show me that their minds have been out to lunch for some time. To them we are just boots (new Marines) who haven't experienced combat yet.

Vietnam is about 1,000 miles long on its coastline. It is widest in North Vietnam, where it reaches almost 350 miles across at one point. This particular area of South Vietnam is constricted in the center to as narrow as 50 miles if measured from the water's edge of the South China Sea, inland to its territorial boundary with Laos. Southernmost South Vietnam is 150 miles wide. Vietnam's total area is 130,000 square miles, and it lies entirely in the tropical zone.

Apart from the large cities of Hanoi in the north and Saigon in the south, and apart from provincial capitals, Vietnam is made up of small villages. Some are in clusters called hamlets. Nearly all of Vietnam's small villages are found on the irrigated plains of the country's two great rivers, the Red River in North Vietnam and the Mekong River in South Vietnam. The villagers gravitate to the riversides, streams, and wells, and work the fields and rice paddies.

Most of the villagers live in small huts built of mud and bamboo with roofs of palm leaves or grass. They sleep on reed mattresses on the ground or on raised platforms. There is no electricity in most villages, so kerosene lamps and candles are used for light in the hours of darkness. There is no such thing as a shopping mall or a department store, and supermarkets don't exist.

The spiritual beliefs of the Vietnamese people are divided mainly among the doctrines and teachings of three great Eastern religions: Confucianism, Taoism, and Buddhism. In each village is a temple, or at least a small shrine.

The Vietnamese people are fiercely independent, with a history of repelling invaders going back a thousand years. As recently as 1945, infringing upon their homeland and mingling in their affairs were French, Japanese, English, Chinese, and Americans, all at the same time.

However glorious the history of this little country and its people has been for the previous thousand years is of no concern to me when I arrive. I decide, in the first hour I am here, that this country is a mess. The Vietnamese people can keep it. Who would want to live here anyway?

1968

As a Marine, I must spend thirteen months in this country before I am eligible to go home. The army's soldiers are required to spend only twelve months. I will be spending all of 1968 and then some in

Vietnam. The only way I can leave before my thirteen months elapse is if I am seriously wounded or, worse, dead and wrapped in a body bag.

It is January 2, 1968—Vietnam's monsoon season. Where there is no hardtop road, there is deep mud. The new arrivals have been ordered to report to a makeshift canvas tent at the side of the airstrip. Two wooden steps ascend to a plywood floor. The canvas walls and roof provide protection from the elements. Judging by the demeanor of the desk sergeant inside, he has seen one too many arriving or departing faces. He is thumbing quickly through the paperwork with my orders and knows exactly what he's looking for. I don't. He finds it.

"Twenty-sixth Marines, huh?"

Somewhere in the pile of papers I have carried to Vietnam, it has been decided that I am assigned to the 26th Marine Regiment, wherever that might be in this godforsaken country. The desk sergeant tells me I will be traveling north and that my regiment is somewhere at the demilitarized zone (DMZ). He says most flights are grounded due to the monsoon's fog and heavy rains and directs me to a temporary barracks, where I will spend the night. Da Nang's airstrip, my port of entry into Vietnam, is the northernmost American base in South Vietnam that is capable of landing a commercial airliner. Farther south are larger bases such as Tan Son Nhut, which is on the outskirts of Saigon; Cam Ranh Bay; and Bien Hoa.

From my barracks in Da Nang, I can see prominent landmarks, such as Monkey Mountain on the peninsula, enclosing the Bay of Da Nang. I see the beginnings of a mountain range that rises to the north, and Route 1, which disappears into a pass called Hai Van. Hai Van Pass goes up the coastline.

Vietnamese people walk freely about the barracks area. They wear black outfits that resemble pajamas. Their heads are covered with cone-shaped straw hats, and on their feet they wear homemade "Ho Chi Minh" sandals, which are cut from discarded rubber tires. The tread is held against their feet with thin strands of rubber or pieces of string. I don't understand why they wear black clothing in such a hot climate. Many Vietnamese adults have black teeth because they chew betel nuts—their form of chewing gum. Unlike chewing gum, the nuts produce a buzz.

Sanitation measures are poor. Dogs, cats, pigs, rats, mice, chickens, ducks, geese, caged birds, and cattle such as water buffalo wander throughout the villages. I see Vietnamese women relieving themselves by just dropping their drawers along the roadside. They make no attempt at modesty.

First Night

It is raining and foggy, so the helicopter ride to the DMZ and my future outfit will wait until tomorrow. Right outside the barracks is a trench for shelter if Da Nang comes under mortar or rocket attack. My assigned cot is complete with mosquito netting. I am tired from my long journey to Vietnam, so I'm going to get some sleep.

Men shouting awaken me. One soldier has also shaken me awake. I don't know how to react, but I think I should at least get out of my cot. One alert soldier, who probably noticed that I am new, directs me to take shelter in the trench outside. There are lots of loud, unfamiliar noises, and several helicopters are flying low above us, their rotor blades loudly slapping the air. I hear explosions and realize that Da Nang is taking incoming enemy rounds. A Marine in the trench says the explosions are from the impacts of enemy 122mm rockets, which are nine feet long. He says the enemy launch them frequently from the foothills west of Da Nang. The helicopters are attempting to find the enemy launch sites.

I am in Vietnam for only a few hours and people are already trying to kill me. The rockets are also exploding in other parts of Da Nang, and I lay in the trench wondering whether anybody is getting killed.

Day Two

While I wait for the pilot to arrive, I sit near the helicopter that will take me north. This morning I was issued combat gear. I signed for a flak jacket, canteen, M16 automatic rifle, several magazines, a bandoleer of ammo, gas mask, poncho, poncho liner, and first-aid and mess kits. Along with those items, I got an air mattress called a rubber lady and several plastic containers of insect repellent that the soldiers call bug juice.

The flak jacket is heavy but necessary. Sewn inside the lining are overlapping layers of fiberglass panels. A front zipper, which runs from waist to neckline, is covered with a flap with several snap fasteners. I have put my vest on using the snaps and not the zipper to allow air to circulate into my chest area. I can already determine how long a Marine has been in Vietnam just by the wear and tear of his flak jacket. If his jacket is torn and stained and the fiberglass panels are out of place, the wearer has been in-country for many months.

My M16 serial number was recorded by the clerk at the supply depot when he issued me the weapon. I am responsible for my weapon. In the Marine Corps you are looked down upon if you misplace your weapon.

I organize my gear while waiting by the helicopter. I have carried several items with me from the United States. In my travel bag I have an inexpensive Mexican steel string guitar and a Mel Bay guitar self-instruction book. I plan to teach myself how to play the guitar if I have time. I keep my guitar out of sight, because I don't want scowls from combat-hardened soldiers who are carrying rifles instead of guitars.

The monsoon is lessening; it is not raining nearly as heavily as it was before. A mud-covered jeep pulls up next to our idle helicopter. The pilot steps from the jeep and, without a word, walks around the helicopter performing a cursory visual inspection of the large aircraft. It is a CH-53, nicknamed the Jolly Green Giant. The pilot gets inside and starts the engine. Still waiting, I watch him through the cockpit window as he checks the gauges and controls; he appears satisfied with his preflight check.

While the pilot inspects the aircraft, another Marine shows up for the flight, and he is friendly. His name is Jeff, and he also has orders to report to the 26th Marine Regiment. I am happy to have company. Small talk between us is interrupted by the pilot, who lowers the back ramp of the chopper and waves us aboard. As we walk up the ramp together, Jeff tells me he is from Philadelphia. He has also just arrived in Vietnam.

I am scared. I don't know how the pilot can see where he's going, because I can't see a thing in this fog. I have never flown in a helicopter before, and I think I like airplanes better. I picture the steel shaft that holds the helicopter's whirling blades to the fuselage and I pray it doesn't snap, because that is what's keeping us from crashing to the ground several thousand feet below.

Making the most of our first helicopter ride, Jeff and I lean out of the open window and look at the summits of mountains as we fly past. The mountain peaks appear as islands protruding from a white sea of fog.

Quang Tri

Our helicopter spirals down in wide circles. The pilot strains to see where he is going. We are landing at a military base in Quang Tri, the capital of South Vietnam's northernmost province, Quang Tri Province. At the base, located less than ten miles from Vietnam's east coast, we will change helicopters, because the pilot says he doesn't like the way this one is performing.

Our new chopper flies us to Dong Ha, an outpost farther north and closer to Vietnam's DMZ, the geographical zone of demarcation established by the Geneva Accords of 1945. The ten-kilometer-wide zone along the seventeenth parallel was to be kept free of all military forces and equipment. The DMZ separates South Vietnam from unfriendly North Vietnam.

It is here in Dong Ha that I will be spending the night. There has been recent incoming, and all the Marines are nervous.

January 4, 1968, Morning

Jeff and I board a military airplane at Dong Ha's airstrip. The C-123 cargo plane, called a Provider, will take us to our assigned regiment, the 26th Marines. The plane has pull-down canvas seats and lots of nylon straps for securing cargo. Jeff and I are again the sole passengers. Where are the rest of those "new guys" who flew with me to Vietnam? How come just Jeff and I are going north to the DMZ? What regiments have the other new guys been assigned to?

The flight crew is congenial. At boarding they invite us to join them in the cockpit, and we spend the flight sitting up front. We can see patches of thick monsoon fog from the airplane's front windows, and here and there I glimpse views of jungle green in breaks in the fog. Vietnam is showing itself to me a little piece at a time.

We have been in the air for only twenty minutes and we are already starting to descend. There is a small airstrip below, and the cockpit compass indicates that we are approaching from the east. I see why this region is called the jungle highlands; some mountain peaks are higher than our plane's wings. We are deep in the highlands now. Looking down I see a river that flows in a valley between the outpost, situated on a plateau, and two towering mountains. It is the Rao Quan River. The pilot says that the two mountain peaks are Hills 950 and 1015. The numbers, representing their height in meters above sea level, are found on topographical maps of this region.

3: Welcome to Khe Sanh

Khe Sanh

Our plane uses the entire length of the runway to land and come to a full stop. Jeff and I have been delivered. This is the outpost that is garrisoned by the 26th Marine Regiment. As we walk down the ramp of the cargo plane, Jeff and I thank the flight crew. Outside the plane, carrying all my belongings, I have the first view of my new home. What minutes ago appeared as a colorful collage from our plane in the sky is now reality. The surrounding valley is breathtaking. I have landed at the biblical Garden of Eden. The only ugly feature is the outpost. The man-made scar atop a plateau is covered with bunkers and airstrip matting, fenced in by barbed and razor wire.

As I glance around my new home and visually absorb as much as possible, my attention is drawn to a structure. For all intents and purposes, it is the base's air traffic control tower. "Tower," it doesn't. Its observation platform is only several feet above my head. It is made of wood, sandbags, and corrugated metal sheets. Wooden ammunition boxes, filled with dirt, are stacked five rows high and painted red. Stenciled on the boxes, in large yellow letters, are the words "WELCOME TO KHE SANH." A smaller sign hanging below the

18

ammo boxes reads "MATCU 62 Airfield Operations." I am learning to read military abbreviations a few at a time. MATCU is short for Marine air traffic control unit.

I stare at the name stenciled on the tower: Khe Sanh. How do I pronounce it? I am overwhelmed with a strange feeling. The name itself is chilling. It feels like a premonition. Something is going to happen here, I just know it.

The outpost is located by an ancient volcano. The soil is a rich red color. In fact, the first Marines I see here are red. The pigment in the red volcanic soil has penetrated their skin.

We present our orders to an officer, who directs us to follow the outpost dirt road going east. Along it, he says, we will find the 26th Marine regimental headquarters. As we walk, the cargo plane that we arrived on rolls down the outpost's airstrip, engines at full throttle. I watch as it reaches takeoff speed and becomes airborne for its flight back to Dong Ha. On the plane are several Marines whose thirteen-month tours in Vietnam are over; that plane is the first of several flights of their journey back to the United States, halfway around the world.

We arrive at the regimental headquarters, and our orders are quickly read. We are told to continue on to the company headquarters to which our orders assign us: Headquarters and Service Company (H&S). Under H&S Company's command is the 81mm mortar platoon, where I am assigned. It is a short walk from regimental headquarters to H&S Company headquarters; already the 81mm mortar emplacements are coming into view. The mortars are in circular gun pits with sandbag walls.

We report to a lieutenant in an underground bunker called the fire directional center (FDC). It is down here that the men receive, gather, and compute compass bearings and distances to targets and use a plotting board to calculate the proper settings (called "dope") to be applied to the mortars gun sights. The compass bearings and distances to targets are transmitted to the FDC by radio from a forward observer (FO), who is outside the outpost in enemy territory. The FDC and FO work from identical field maps. Forward observers have a choice of weapons; they can request a strike on an enemy position from mortars, artillery, or fighter jets. The 81mm mortars respond within one minute. Our mortar squads are in direct radio communication with the FDC, which is in direct communication with the FO. The 81mm mortar fires in all directions. The high angle of fire allows it to fire over a mountain. The mortars themselves are set in place, compass oriented, to the same terrain that is illustrated on the maps of the FO and FDC.

We have several mortar emplacements on the perimeter. We call our mortars "guns." The lieutenant in the fire directional center assigns me to gun #1 and Jeff to the squad at gun #2. Four 81mm guns are set up in circular sandbagged gun pits at the eastern perimeter and in other mortar positions elsewhere on the outpost. I hurry over to gun #1 and report to my squad leader, Jake, a Marine from Pittsburgh. Jake welcomes me aboard.

I look out from our gun pit; we have lots of open ground that rolls down from our position. A trench line separates us from enemy territory; it is dug along and behind our circular strands of razor and barbed wire defenses. The trench line is manned by Bravo Company, 1st Battalion, 26th Marines. Bravo Company and we form the first line of defense for this section of the post perimeter. Not doubt about it, I have a ringside seat.

I am introduced to the gunner, Bill, from Pennsylvania. It seems that everybody I have met so far in Vietnam is from Pennsylvania. Our squad leader, Jake, tells me he has two Purple Hearts; he has been wounded in combat twice already. He says he is hoping to get wounded one more time, a minor wound, just enough to draw blood. Three times wounded gets you out of Nam. It is a ticket home.

Jake is pointing out others in the mortar section who have Purple Hearts and tells me to respect them because "they've been there." All this talk about Purple Hearts is starting to worry me.

After I am introduced to other Marines and become familiar with the squad's gun procedures, I relax and view the beautiful scenery in the distance. As I gaze at the surrounding valley, it finally sinks in that I am here. I am a member of the 1st Battalion, 26th Marine Regiment. I am also anxious.

There are three battalions in my 26th Marine Regiment. Each battalion is composed of four rifle companies. The 1st and 3d Battalions of the regiment are assigned to the outpost and several surrounding strategic hilltop positions. The 26th Marines belonged to the 5th Marine Division during World War II and has been reactivated for the Vietnam War; it came here in 1966. The last time all three battalions of the 26th Marines fought together was on Iwo Jima in 1945. In Vietnam the 26th Marines operates under the jurisdiction of the 3d Marine Division.

At Khe Sanh, several miles from the country of Laos, the DMZ, and the Ho Chi Minh Trail, my regiment is responsible for holding the combat base, and positions on the tops of Hills 881S, 861A, 558, and 950. These hills strategically dominate and overlook enemy infiltration routes into South Vietnam, which are collectively called the Ho Chi Minh Trail.

Here in the northern highlands of South Vietnam is a section of the Annamese Mountains that begins at North Vietnam's border with China and curves down through the length of Vietnam. Some of the mountain peaks tower thousands of feet above sea level. A Montagnard tribe called the Bru dwell in these highlands. Millennia ago the ground on which I am standing was the crater of a giant volcano. The rich red soil is all that remains from the many, now-long-silent eruptions. This pigmented soil permeates the skin and eventually turns it red. The rich soil nurtures any form of vegetation, and there is even a coffee plantation nearby. In one glance I take in many prominent terrain features.

All this awesome topography—the high mountains, the plateaus, the deep valleys, the rivers and streams—are instrumental in producing this region's unique weather, called the *crachin* (French word for "spit"). The *crachin* is produced by a combination of the topography and the tropical daytime heat, the coolness of highland nights, the triple-canopy jungle, and the heavy tropical rains of the monsoon season. Fog and clouds continually form. Sometimes the clouds conceal mountaintops, and the fog rolls up from the river valley and blankets the plateau outpost until the heat from the late-morning sun finally burns it off. Late in the afternoon, as the temperature drops, fog rolls back out of the valley and again covers the Khe Sanh outpost.

There is plenty of fish to catch and wildlife to hunt in this region; there are also elephants, pythons, and king cobras. Tigers have been here a long time. The name of a nearby mountain attests to that; the villagers call it Tiger Tooth Mountain.

Khe Sanh Airstrip

In the midst of this breathtaking Eden is Khe Sanh's most prominent man-made feature, our airstrip. The tarmac is built atop a bed of crushed basaltic rock thrown up from the extinct volcano. The original runway was constructed by the army's Special Forces several years earlier. It was originally made of Marston mats, which are interlocking sections of steel matting perforated with many small circular holes. The holes allow the stone and soil upon which the mat is laid to flow through, then be compacted and graded. Any excess is plowed to the sides.

Military engineers have upgraded the runway. They have bulldozed the old matting with the holes in it and laid down solid steel interlocking sections with no holes. There are large scrap piles of the old crumpled, twisted airstrip matting scattered around the outpost. One pile is about fifty yards from our gun pit.

Our outpost is astride Route 9, an early explorers' route. Some sections are no wider than my parents' driveway. Route 9 heads east from here past the Rockpile, Camp Carroll, and Cam Lo before eventually reaching Dong Ha, a port city on South Vietnam's coast. Route 9 west goes into Laos. Route 9 is, at the moment, impassable in places because of washouts caused by the torrential rains. Route 9 is dangerous because it is easily susceptible to ambush.

The New Guys

At the gun pits Jeff and I are the news of the day. A Marine who has just arrived from America is a big event here. It's a happening. You can't hide the fact, because your new, spotless jungle utilities and boots give you away; so does the new cloth camouflage cover on your steel combat helmet, your new canteen cover, and your new gas mask pouch. It is like wearing a clean football jersey. We new guys are asked lots of questions: "Where are you from?" "What's going on back in the world?"

I am the new kid on the block. I don't have any friends yet, and I don't know the neighborhood. After numerous helicopter and plane rides to get here, I don't even know where "here" is. I am paradoxically both a drawback and an asset, a soldier with no seniority. I am a mere replacement lacking combat experience and I am assigned menial tasks such as burning the shitters, which are fifty-five-gallon steel drums cut in half and placed beneath wooden seats. They are the outpost toilets. Their contents are soaked with diesel fuel daily and burned for sanitary measures at all outposts in Vietnam. Burning shitters is just one chore; filling sandbags is another. I am a Green Marine (newly arrived in Vietnam) and will be assigned undesirable watches during the night. It will be my duty to perform tasks bequeathed to me by the previous new guy. The previous new guy might have arrived a month, a week, or even a day before me, but he arrived before me. My arriving in Vietnam after him now gives that Marine his first degree of seniority—seniority over me.

First Night

As we watch the sun go down over Khe Sanh for the first time, Jeff and I are issued woolen blankets and told that the Hawk—the cool wind of Vietnam's highlands—will be out tonight. I am assigned a rack inside a hooch (soldier's dwelling) below ground level. Its roof is fortified with timbers, soil-packed wooden ammunition boxes, and layer upon layer of dirt-filled sandbags.

There are four places to sleep in the hooch: collapsible canvas military cots on the dirt floor and positioned against the hooch's north and south earthen walls, and canvas stretchers, suspended above the cots and secured to the ceiling timbers by ropes tied to their handles. Apart from their use in carrying battlefield casualties, the stretchers are places to sleep. As the new guy, I am assigned one of the stretchers. It is accessible only by using the cot below as a step.

As I lie on my stretcher on the threshold of sleep, my last conscious thought is one of pride in being a member of the 26th Marine Regiment. I fall asleep staring at the canopy of a camouflage parachute, which is nailed to the roof timbers of the bunker ceiling to keep the dirt in sandbags on the roof from falling into our faces. I will sleep soundly. It has been a long journey from that recruiting booth in a Nanuet, New York, shopping plaza to here.

Khe Sanh, tucked into the Vietnamese highlands, is a place few people in the world outside of this province of Quang Tri have ever heard of. This remote place, whose spelling and pronunciation seem odd, is now my home. As I sleep, I am unaware that my foreboding impressions upon arrival are real. Just two days ago, events unfolded on the combat base perimeter that will lead to others and will put Khe Sanh into history books, and my 26th Marine Regiment along with it.

The Dog

After dark on January 2, six enemy soldiers disguised in Marine uniforms approach the base perimeter on the other side of the outpost to scout our defensive positions. The Lima Company Marines on night watch are alerted to the enemy soldiers' approach by the barking of their sentry dog. The Marines initially hesitate to shoot because the enemy soldiers are wearing Marine uniforms. The sentries shout out a challenge, but the seconds pass without a response from the figures dressed in Marine uniforms, so the sentries open fire. The soldiers are North Vietnamese. One of them, though bleeding heavily from his wounds, manages to retrieve a map case from a wounded comrade and escape, leaving a trail of blood as he flees into the jungle tree line. Because of that incident, our base is on red alert, the highest state of readiness. We anticipate further trouble.

"On the Guns"

Someone is shouting into the entranceway of our hooch, commanding us to go to our mortar's gun pit. "On the guns! On the guns!" Alert now and in the gun pit, I look into the darkness. At periodic intervals we fire illumination rounds with time settings that make them explode just a few hundred feet from our position.

Once a round is ignited, brilliant candlepower falls slowly to the ground attached to a tiny parachute before finally landing and burning out. The brightness provides sufficient light to visually detect any enemy soldiers who might be just outside our perimeter. But once the light is extinguished, we are momentarily blinded due to spoiled night vision from looking at the flare.

Directly in front of our gun emplacement, on the base's eastern perimeter, is an area of waist-high grass. Carefully laid trip flares and antipersonnel mines have transformed this area, literally, into a no-man's-land. Enemy soldiers have a reputation for their courage and uncanny ability to penetrate such defenses.

For more than two hours I have been waiting and anticipating seeing my foe face-to-face for the first time. It has not happened. We are standing down (going off alert status). Several of us have been granted permission to return to our hooches, and we try to go back to sleep.

Morning

I am awake at first light and discover the base alive with rumors. The scuttlebutt says that the papers found on the dead enemy officers identify them as high-ranking members of a North Vietnamese regiment known to be in the region. We don't need the commander over American forces in Vietnam, General Westmoreland, or Col. David Lownds, our regimental commander, to tell us that the enemy reconnaissance of our lines is a sure sign of what's to come. We can figure that out for ourselves.

This is my first morning at the combat base. As a newcomer I am scheduled for orientation at 0900. I will be told exactly where we are geographically and what mission we are to accomplish. The meeting is being held in a tent along the dirt road that runs parallel to the airstrip. This road is the outpost's Main Street. On the way I see several structures that arouse my curiosity. On the north side of this road is a tent with its canvas sides raised to reveal several cots. Rows of sandbags, layered one atop another to three feet high, outline the tent's perimeter and are meant to protect personnel from the shrapnel of mortar, rocket, or artillery rounds, although no protection would help in a direct hit. Next on my walk I see a plywood structure with a corrugated metal roof. The roof has sandbags scattered here and there to keep it weighted down in the event of a sudden strong wind. The walls are fortified with sandbags, the same as the tent containing the cots. At the front of the building is a red wooden sign with a skull-and-crossbones insignia painted in white. The sign reads "RECON: THE EYES AND EARS OF THE 26TH MARINE REGIMENT." The fence in front of this structure, which borders the base's dirt road, consists of metal posts strung with three strands of barbed wire with a foot of spacing between the strands. Continuing in a westerly direction along the road, I encounter more tents fortified in the same way. Several passageways lead to subterranean rooms. Their rooftops are heavily padded with sandbags and other protective materials that their builders have scrounged. Some of the roofs are nearly ten feet thick with sandbags and fortifying materials.

The next hut is the mess hall, which is less a hall than a shelter to protect the cooks from adverse weather as they prepare hot meals or stacks of sandwiches. The structure is crudely framed and sheathed with plywood; corrugated metal sheets form the roof. Outside the mess hall, against and nearly touching one of its walls, are four large propane cylinders that feed the flames for the stoves. In the open cupboard inside are gallon-sized cans of rations. All the cans are painted uniform military green. In the military even a can of peaches has a serial number; everything is identified by numbers and letters. If I could see what was printed on the cans in the cupboard of the mess hall, it would read something like this: "Peaches; Peaches, Yellow; Total weight of Peaches; Total weight of Peaches and can; Serial number of Peaches," and so forth. The military is very descriptive. Even I have a serial number.

Farther west along the road, on the south shoulder, are three small generators mounted on single-axle trailers. Nearby is a larger box-shaped generator. Sandbags are stacked and sloped against its military green sheet-metal housing. Aside from providing electricity to power lightbulbs in some command bunkers, the large generator produces a sonorous noise, which seems out of place. I will soon learn to give these generators a wide berth when passing. Farther along the base road, the airstrip widens to allow planes and helicopters to unload or take on cargo without disrupting other aircraft from taking off and landing.

Off to the side of this widened area is a red fire truck. It looks naked, stripped of all but the basic tools of its trade. It doesn't have as many fire hoses, bells, sirens, and lights as stateside fire trucks, and its red paint is covered with a film of red Khe Sanh dust. The truck looks out of place, parked in the open without a firehouse.

There is much to see on this first walk around the outpost. There are several water sources mounted on single-axle trailers, called water buffaloes. There are additional water sources called lister bags, which are canvas bags suspended on tripods. A Marine can fill his canteen at a lister bag by opening the spigot at its base.

I have walked past several jeeps, and one jeep parked in front of a headquarters bunker has neatly stenciled letters that read "Mission Commander."

More important to me than the structures are the weapons. There are several tanks, whose lethal appearance gives me a feeling of relief. An armored vehicle, which appears more frightening than the tanks, has tracks and mounts six 106mm recoilless rifles; it is called an *ontos* (Greek word for "thing"). There are several mules, which are four-wheel motorized cargo platforms; some of the mules have been modified and carry 106mm recoilless rifles bolted to their platforms. The mules without armament are used to move cargo.

One artillery piece along the base perimeter has the name "Ban Shee" painted on its barrel in red. The two-wheeled 105mm howitzer stands on an octagon-shaped concrete slab inside a large circular gun pit. The protective walls of Ban Shee's gun pit are the height of three wooden ammo boxes and one sandbag, all packed with dirt. The diameter of this artillery gun pit makes it a large target; I wouldn't want to be a member of its gun crew during incoming fire. It is too large a bull's-eye.

These sites are my first detailed look at the Khe Sanh Combat Base. Khe Sanh is in the northernmost area of the I Corps tactical zone, which consists of five provinces.

Khe Sanh is close to the demilitarized zone, which separates North and South Vietnam. We are less than ten miles from South Vietnam's border with Laos. There has been a lot of fighting in the hills. In fact, there have been so many battles that they are collectively called the Hill Fights. The enemy are the regular army of the North Vietnamese.

When jungle-fighting in this region, as within most of Vietnam, the trail you were ambushed on yesterday could be and often is the trail you will be ambushed on today or tomorrow or the day after, until you are finally wounded or killed or are fortunate enough to survive ambushes for the duration of your tour. When your tour in Vietnam is finally over, a new guy will come along, replace you, and walk down those same surprise-filled jungle paths. When the gunfire has ended, your outfit might have inflicted more wounded and killed on the enemy than the enemy have inflicted on you, but you have no territorial gains to show for it. The territory wasn't yours to keep. It immediately goes back up for grabs.

Marines who go out on patrols in this region call it the Badlands. The enemy are the disciplined, well-equipped, and highly professional North Vietnamese Army (NVA), which is collectively addressed as Mister Charles; that is a sign of respect over the Viet Cong, who are simply called Charlie.

When you enlist in the Marine Corps, you begin rank as a private. After military training, just before being sent to Vietnam, a Marine is normally promoted to private first class if he has not earned the rank already. Big deal. Perhaps the Marines grant this promotion to give a man a better feeling about himself before going off to battle. "Private First Class" has more eye appeal on a tombstone than just "Private." Though I am only a private, I am smart enough to realize that trouble is coming to Khe Sanh. We are isolated, and we are sitting on the doorstep of enemy North Vietnam.

Scuttlebutt spreading about the base tells of increased enemy movement on the Ho Chi Minh Trail. This infiltration route leads the enemy from North Vietnam and penetrates deep into South Vietnam by way of Laos and Cambodia. The trail is just several miles to the west. Rumors also tell of enemy troops massing in the immediate vicinity of our base. Apprehension is in the air; being a new guy, I am probably the most apprehensive of all.

Orientation

Jeff and I arrive at the orientation tent. There are several other soldiers present, all new, all fresh from the States, all assigned to their companies on the combat base. Everyone is seated and staring at a map pinned to the wall. The map is marked with a red felt-tipped pen. The red marks form a circular pattern, and in the middle of this circle is a black dot.

Something is wrong; no one is smiling. It is very quiet, as in a church or a funeral parlor. A Marine officer enters the tent; his demeanor is all business. "Good morning, Marines. Welcome to Khe Sanh. Welcome to the Twenty-sixth Marine Regiment. Glad to have you aboard."

He goes right to the wall map, stands to the side, thrusts his arm up, and points to the black dot in the center of all the red marks. He raises his voice to ensure we all hear. "This black dot is your present location: Khe Sanh. These red marks surrounding the dot represent North Vietnamese Army divisions and regimental-size units. We are, at this moment, surrounded. Intelligence informs us that it's just a matter of time before the enemy will strike. I'm ordering you to return immediately to your assigned companies and start digging. Dig in. Dig in now."

Jeff and I look at each other in disbelief. We leave the tent and return down the base road to our mortar section. We walk fast, and there is no conversation. We are both stunned. I am not looking at the base's scenery on my return trip; there is more on my mind now, and it is not sight-seeing. I chastise myself as I walk. "So I joined the Marines because I wanted adventure, huh?" If it were physically possible, I would kick myself really hard in the butt.

81mm Mortar Section, Eastern Perimeter

The men in my mortar section are in a frenzy of activity. They just received the same situation report. I am angry. Great timing, I don't have. Here I am: A week hasn't passed since my arrival in Vietnam and I am in a country where American soldiers wrestle rock apes to have fun. Where water buffalo instead of Massey-Ferguson tractors are used to plow farm fields. Where you are doing fine if there are no leeches swimming in your canteen water. Where you need to carry a bottle of mosquito repellent. Where pizza doesn't exist, and if it did, delivery would be impossible. Here I am, surrounded by North Vietnam's best.

Digging In

There is a substantial amount of digging to be done. Existing trench lines must be deepened and lengthened. The sandbag walls of each circular gun pit need to be raised higher with several more layers of soil-filled bags. This additional height increases our protection from shrapnel in the event of a near miss by an enemy shell. In addition to these tasks, each man must dig his own foxhole. These fighting holes will serve as a place to sleep while providing a position of relative safety from which to observe our perimeter. The holes will also be our fighting positions to defend the combat base when and if the enemy attack. Bravo Company's trench lines are the first defensive positions that the enemy will encounter if they attack at the eastern perimeter of our outpost. Our gun pits are located behind their line.

In each Marine's 782 gear (field equipment) is a small shovel called an entrenching tool. Now, considering what was said at our orientation, I think the shovel is much too small. I can't dig as much or as fast as I would like. I feel as though I am digging with a spoon.

We are working together, excavating dirt from the trench lines, shoveling it into sandbags, then stacking the bags one on another to raise the walls of our gun pit and fortify the walls and roof of nearby ammunition bunkers. Using the small shovel is an exercise in frustration.

The digging along our positions has continued in earnest for several days. Now, finally, the time has come to dig my own foxhole somewhere near our mortar pits. My position in the squad as an ammo man requires that I be ready for gun action at all times. My squad leader told me to dig my fighting hole between a small ammunition bunker and our mortar's gun pit. He selected this area because it will be my job, when the time comes, to carry boxes of high-explosive mortar rounds from the small ammunition bunker to our mortar's gun crew. Each wooden ammo box contains three mortar projectiles. The wooden boxes have rope handles; when the boxes are needed, I will be delivering them on the run to the gun pit. There I am to open each box, remove the mortar rounds, and unpack each round from its wrappings. The older stores of mortar rounds are encased in cylindrical hard black cardboard tubes. Recently manufactured mortar rounds are packaged in a rigid plastic cylinder with a screw-off top. Once I unwrap the mortar rounds, I am responsible for removing the safety mechanisms to arm the finned bombs. This done, if required, I can adjust the distance the mortar projectile can travel by removing one or several of the bags of black-powder propellant charges, called increments, which are attached to the bomb's tail assembly. Then I will run back to the ammo bunker, retrieve another box of ammunition, and repeat the cycle.

Surveying the level ground where I have been ordered to dig my fighting hole, I am undecided as to the spot where I will begin digging. I decide to let fate determine this. Picking up a small chip of discarded wood from the ground nearby, I face north and, while looking up at Hills 950 and 1015, throw the wood chip over my shoulder. Where the wood chip lands, I will dig.

I dig to a depth of nearly four feet. The foxhole viewed from above looks like the letter H. One leg is an open rectangular pit, distant from but parallel to our barbed wire perimeter. This front section has no roof; I will be completely exposed to the weather in this open part, but I can observe any action at the eastern perimeter of the combat base. I will also be able to observe the eastern end of the airstrip. The airstrip is to my left when I face east toward our perimeter, looking out over our lines and into the valley. It is this front part of my fighting hole that I will occupy to face the enemy if they attack our perimeter.

The other leg of my H-shaped foxhole I dig to the same depth but, because it is the rear section, it will have a roof. I construct it out of discarded wooden cargo pallets and a layer of discarded metal airstrip matting. Then I add several layers of sandbags, on which I stack a layer of discarded wooden ammo boxes, each filled with so much soil that I can barely close the lid. Here in the fortified roofed section is where I will sleep if the fighting starts at Khe Sanh. The crossbar of the H serves as a roofed passageway, so I can come out of the rain without having to crawl all the way back into the roofed section.

It has taken two days of work to complete my foxhole. After contemplating finishing touches to spruce up my new home, I lay a single layer of sandbags along the edges of the open section in order to have fabric to sit or lean on rather than bare ground. I construct sandbag steps that lead from the foxhole's dirt floor to ground level. This makes my entrance and exit easier.

I place a wooden ammunition box inside the rear section; I will store my few personal belongings here. I position another wooden ammo box in the front section, which I will use as a place to sit. I scrounge a piece of discarded tent canvas and make a curtain for my passageway—a door of sorts.

My fighting hole is now complete. It reminds me what old Mrs. Maxwell never failed to tell me after an afternoon of pulling weeds in her yard. "Now, John, you should always take a moment to stand back, look at, and admire your work once you've completed it." The old gal never paid very well, but she provided lots of Irish tea breaks and was always quick to offer words of wisdom. I never liked having to stand alongside her, admiring a flower patch that had just been ripped free of weeds. I just wanted her to pay up for the hours that I worked so I could get out of her yard and go find my friends. She really was a pleasant old lady, but it always seemed that when I needed pocket money the most, she paid me off in plums.

But on this day, my foxhole completed, I am heeding old Mrs. Maxwell's advice. I stand back and gaze at my workmanship. I look at the layers of varied protective materials that I have piled on the roof. The top of my fortification looks like a giant club sandwich made of dirt. But I should have added more sandbags. Other Marines have painstakingly and meticulously fortified their fighting holes, preparing for the worst-case scenario. We have all used ammo boxes and sandbags, which are here in abundance, but several Marines scrounged expended brass artillery casings and placed them upright, side by side atop the roof of their fighting hole. They filled the brass canisters with soil and compacted it, hoping it will provide added protection from a direct hit by an enemy round. They hope the soil-packed metal casings will detonate the enemy shell before it can penetrate their foxhole's roof and explode inside their hole with them inside.

As I look at other Marines' fighting holes, I see that theirs have twice as many layers of sandbags and wooden ammo boxes on top of their roofs. Their efforts, to me, seem futile. Though I have no combat experience, I know what damage a direct hit from an artillery round can do. I have seen artillery fired in Marine training. The paltry efforts I put forth in the construction of my foxhole are a reflection of my thoughts on the subject. Our sandbagged rooftops might stop a small enemy 61mm mortar round, but a direct hit by a rocket or an artillery round will blow the entire foxhole to smithereens along with anyone who is unfortunate enough to be in it. Compared to other foxholes, mine appears downright naked. Even if my foxhole took a direct hit, more layers of sandbags would just delay the outcome by a fraction of a second. The only thing that can help in the event of a direct hit is to not be inside the foxhole when the round strikes and explodes.

For those of us living here, whose responsibility it is to keep our base out of enemy hands, our living or dying or being wounded is really in fate's hands, not ours.

4: West Dickens Avenue

My Fighting Hole

While scrounging the area for discarded materials to fortify my fighting hole, I come across a pile of junk. I find spent shell casings, a green metal ammo box with a handle on its lid, a gas mask with a broken eye lens, and some discarded C-ration cans. Beneath this pile of junk I notice a piece of bright yellow metal. Curious, I pull it out from under the pile and see an object that seems completely incongruous with Khe Sanh. I have found a metal street sign, the same type that is erected on almost every street corner in every town and city in the United States. The yellow sign has black letters that read "W DICKENS AV." The "W" tells me this sign was once located on a street corner in the western part of whatever city or town it came from. I hold the metal sign with both hands and read it as though it has as much to say as a newspaper. I wonder about the place it came from, and I wish, no matter where that is, that I was there instead of here.

It seems odd that someone would carry a street sign all the way to this place in the mountain highlands of Vietnam. Then again, I think I am odd for dragging a guitar all the way to this remote outpost.

I assume that the sign must have a significant meaning for its previous owner. Perhaps it is the street where he grew up; perhaps it was shipped to him by buddies in his neighborhood as a morale booster after he arrived in Vietnam. I will make use of this sign.

I cut a piece of wood from one of the ammo boxes and whittle it into a pointed stake with my bayonet. I extract several of the nails that fasten the box together, use my small shovel for a hammer, and pound the wooden stake into the ground at the front left corner of my fighting hole. The sign has a metal mounting bracket with four predrilled holes. How convenient. Through the holes I insert the nails and hammer them firmly, securing the sign to the wooden stake. My sign is now erected. With this simple act, my previously nameless, personality-less, and featureless hole in the earth is no longer nameless, personality-less, and featureless. With this seemingly inane act, everything about my hole has changed. Now I have a home with an address: West Dickens Avenue, Khe Sanh.

An hour hasn't passed since I put up the sign. A Marine approaches my foxhole and notices the sign. He says West Dickens Avenue is a major thoroughfare in Chicago. Another Marine comes over and says that West Dickens Avenue is a major street in New York City. I am still not sure what city the sign came from, but at least the name has more personality than "Avenue A" or "C Street."

Sitting in my foxhole and admiring my sign, I remember the day we had orientation, and I recall the wall map with the red circles that surrounded the little black dot that represents our combat base's position here, near the enemy border. These sobering thoughts make me realize that I am sitting on a volcano, literally and figuratively.

Recent Past

The 1st Battalion, 26th Marine Regiment, of which I am now a member, has been on combat operations in this region since the spring of 1967. The regiment was sent here as a relief force to assist the 3d and 12th Marine Regiments, which in turn had come to assist the 9th Marine Regiment. All these Marine regiments have battled with

the North Vietnamese Army, whose objective is to launch diver-
sionary attacks on military outposts in the extreme northern region
of South Vietnam. The main objective of the North Vietnamese Army
is to overrun South Vietnam cities such as Dong Ha, Quang Tri, Hue,
and Phu Bai. These cities are to our rear, south, and east. The few
scattered military outposts in the region are primarily fire support
bases or artillery emplacements, and they have designated names
prefixed by "Camp" or "Firebase" or "LZ" (landing zone). Several of
the outposts are so small that a helicopter has barely enough room
to land. All outposts have a name in Vietnam. All outposts are situated on strategic terrain such as a hilltop or at a place from which
the base's artillery can be aimed on suspected enemy positions and
infiltration routes. Most outposts are regularly called upon by
Marines in the jungle on patrol to fire artillery rounds into enemy
positions. It is a comforting thought to know that you can request
help from guns that are miles away.

When a request for artillery support from men in contact with
the enemy is received at one of these outposts, the impacts of the
first shots fired are visually observed, then verbal adjustments are
relayed via the patrol's radio to bring the artillery fire dead on target. Adjustments such as "up a hundred yards," "down fifty yards,"
"right seventy-five yards" are transmitted until the artillery shells
strike the intended target. Then the order "Fire for effect" is relayed, and the guns fire until ordered to stop. The outposts most
talked about at Khe Sanh are Camp Carroll and the Rockpile. Their
guns can fire explosives into any area immediately surrounding our
position.

What the NVA has thus far not been able to accomplish still remains on their combat agenda. The buildup is on for both the enemy and for us. Both sides are preparing for what is expected to
come in this first month of 1968: more fighting.

I have an excellent view of the Khe Sanh airstrip. Cargo planes
and helicopters fly in daily with pallets of ammunition, medical
supplies, fuel, and food. Also arriving are bundles and bundles of
new sandbags. Looking at all the sandbags we have been shipped

for building fortifications, I wish that they came prefilled. I am sick of shoveling dirt into bags.

We know that the North Vietnamese will attack; we just don't know when. We are making all the necessary preparations. We preregister our mortar by firing at areas on the map that we feel the enemy might use, such as trails and possible enemy assembly areas. We register our mortar fire and mark down the coordinates of many locations along the rivers and creeks, hoping that these will be places where the enemy might bathe or fill their canteens. We register fire on the places we feel the enemy might soon be if they are not there already. We practice firing high-explosive mortar rounds to impact right in front of our own lines in preparation for a possible ground attack against our perimeter. We fire in so close to our own gun pit that if our gun's barrel was at a higher angle, we would blow ourselves up.

We prepare as best we can. I can see trenches connected to trenches, trenches connected to ammo bunkers, trenches leading to mortar gun pits, and trenches leading to our individual fighting holes. I notice the absence of one trench we should have dug but didn't, a trench that would protect someone who had to go to the nearby outhouse.

Our earthworks are complete. Our guns are registered. It appears that we are prepared for the worst. At least we think we are.

The Enemy

Several days have passed since the completion of our preparations. Intelligence concerning enemy troops is becoming chillingly explicit. We find out that amassing in the vicinity of Khe Sanh is the 325th Division, which is positioning itself just north of Hill 881. We discover that the 304th Division is making its new home immediately southwest of us. We confirm that the 320th Division is just north of the Rockpile, the fire support base. We now know that elements of the NVA 324th Division are grouping at the DMZ just to the north of us. We receive lots of bad news, and there is no good news.

We are six thousand strong, all present and accounted for, but our numbers are divided and spread among positions on surrounding strategic hilltops and the combat base itself. I find myself frequently looking around and wishing there were more of us. The estimated enemy strength is at least twenty to thirty thousand troops. Whatever their numbers, I don't intend to walk outside of our lines and take a head count. But this is the Marine Corps. Historically, we have always shown up for battles a little shorthanded.

All these grim reports about the enemy buildup have made me sure of two things. I will definitely get the adventure I was seeking when I enlisted, whether I want it or not; and I am sure that I have no choice in this matter, because I can't just pack my bags and leave.

Waiting

While waiting for the unknown, we, the encircled, ease into a daily routine, which begins in the morning at the makeshift mess hall where a hot breakfast can be obtained, with a possibility of seconds if there are any leftovers.

After breakfast one can stop at the conex box that serves as our area's PX (post exchange). Unlike post exchanges found on large military bases that offer as many items for sale as a stateside department store, our PX carries only basics such as toothpaste, shaving gear, soap, and the like. It also sells film.

Another one of these conex boxes, which are corrugated steel containers with two doors on the front, serves as our post office. Several feet away is a wooden ammo box placed on end; mail can be deposited through a sawed-out opening. Mail collection hours are stenciled on the door of the box: 0830 for the morning pickup and 1400 for the final pickup of the day.

I find it odd that the wooden box lists the hours of mail collection. It is not as if the mailbox is the terminus of an extensive mail route. It is not standing on the corner of Broadway and Main in Busyville, USA. All the Marine mailman must do to fetch the mail from the box is walk about ten feet and open the door of the ammo box.

I have already learned that the best mail service in Vietnam is provided by the crew chief or the door gunner on any helicopter that lands near you. Take your letter and run up to the window of the chopper and hand it to a member of the crew. Just keep your head low and watch out for the chopper's whirling blades. If you happen to run into them, the letter you are mailing will be your last. You can always count on the chopper crews to put the letter in motion immediately.

Showering

We don't shower every day, only when we feel we need to. We use water sparingly. It has to be hand-carried in five-gallon jerry cans to our positions. Unequaled in Yankee ingenuity and architecture are the outhouses and the showers.

Our shower facility, just yards from our mortar gun pits, consists of an upright fifty-five-gallon steel drum atop a roughly constructed wooden frame. There is just enough head clearance for a man to stand under it. The top of the drum is completely cut away. The bottom has been shot full of holes by an automatic weapon. The bullet holes allow the water to pour down in little streamlets. The water is supplied by another Marine who carries a five-gallon jerry can filled with water up a wooden ladder. When you are ready, he pours the water from the jerry can into the open end of the steel drum, and you are on your way to cleanliness. A good shower takes two trips up the ladder, or ten gallons. When your shower is complete, you switch rolls.

The outhouse structure is unique, too. The lower part is sheathed with plywood. The upper half is screened, ostensibly to keep out flies. The screening is superfluous, because the flies follow you in the moment you open the door. Inside, running the width of the structure, is a wooden platform with a hole cut into it. Beneath the hole is a halved fifty-five-gallon steel drum, which serves as a waste receptacle. We call these structures shitters.

The waste accumulated within the half drums is sanitized daily. The drums are pulled out from underneath the platform; then a generous amount of diesel fuel is poured onto them and set ablaze. Diesel fuel takes longer to ignite than gasoline or kerosene. The Marine who ignites the fuel must stand there with a wick of burning paper or wood and hold the flame to the fuel until it ignites. Once ignited, the burning contents spew forth thick black smoke and an odor that permeates not only the combat base but the whole valley. The odor of diesel fuel continually lingers in the air here. All outposts in Vietnam reek of burning human excrement and diesel fuel. There's always a shitter burning somewhere.

Tactics

The digging of defensive positions is not what the Marines have trained me for. The Corps didn't instruct us on how to build a bunker or dig a trench line. I didn't fill one single sandbag in Marine training. We did learn that it is best to dig a foxhole when we are setting up positions for an overnight stay, but not with the intent of living in it indefinitely.

We were trained to attack and destroy, to always be the aggressor, to never spend a second night on the same piece of real estate when there is more to attack.

My Foxhole

One reason I didn't dig West Dickens Avenue deeper is because I didn't relish the thought of digging my own grave. Within my freshly excavated hole in the ground, marked with my street sign, I have stowed all my worldly possessions, which aren't many. I have several pairs of military issue green tube socks, several pairs of underwear, a field jacket, and a spare pair of green jungle utilities—a pair of trousers and a long-sleeved shirt. I have no civilian clothes with me. They are hanging in a closet at my parent's home back in the States.

The remainder is stuffed in my seabag, warehoused in Okinawa. In that bag is a pair of loafers, a pair of trousers, and two shirts. I could have brought them with me, but I didn't see the wisdom of carrying them around Vietnam in anticipation of wearing them for a few days on R and R. Besides, when my chance eventually comes to take an R and R, those clothes will no longer fit. I will be slimmer due to weight loss from living in Vietnam's tropical heat.

In the back of my foxhole I have stored my guitar and instruction book. The only remaining personal possession I have is a small pocket address book, which contains telephone numbers of several of my friends in the States. I see now how pointless it is for me to have their telephone numbers. I haven't seen a single phone since the day I landed in Vietnam.

I have a book with me: a paperback novel by John le Carré called *The Looking Glass War.* The book has nothing to do with the Vietnam War, though in many ways the title could have. The Vietnam War is a looking-glass war. The American press receives daily news releases that keep the media up to date on events here. The American public can also see the war on color film footage, with sound effects, by watching television.

I have stocked up on bottles of bug juice (insect repellent) to help ward off Vietnam's huge mosquito population. I carry one bottle at all times. Another important possession is my P-38, which is not a weapon but a tiny one-moveable-part can opener. In Vietnam, a Marine becomes attached to a can opener, usually the first one he uses while in-country. Some soldiers even wear one around their neck on their dog tag chain. I am not emotionally attached to the first can opener I used. Every case of C rations has a handful of new openers inside the box.

I also have some drugs: halazone tablets for sterilizing the water in my canteen (although giving it a terrible taste) and malaria pills, which we take regularly. We are supposed to swallow them the moment they are handed to us. The navy doc, a corpsman, watches to make sure we take them, but I have a stash, because I never swallow them. They taste terrible. We are issued salt tablets to help us not dehydrate in Vietnam's heat. In addition, I have atropine syringes. They are needles set in a small vial containing a serum with which we would inject ourselves in the event of a nerve-gas attack. I have several needles. I keep them out of my sight, because I don't need a visible reminder of the possibility of a nerve-gas attack. I have never liked needles to begin with. Once I fainted at the sight of one.

I don't have any money with me. What money I do have $50 is deposited at the Marine Midland Bank in Nyack. The only reason I have an account at all was because the bank advertised that anyone opening a new account with $50 or more would receive a free gift. The choice was a toaster or an umbrella. I selected the umbrella. It didn't survive the first rainstorm.

I have journeyed from Nyack, New York, to Parris Island, South Carolina, to Camps Geiger and Lejeune in North Carolina, to Camp Pendleton in California, to Anchorage, Alaska, to Okinawa, to Da Nang, to Dong Ha, to Khe Sanh, to this hole in the ground. I have come a long way. Or have I? If I hadn't joined the Marines, I would be sleeping in a big beautiful bedroom back in the States instead of in a hole. For better or worse, I am here and all moved in. West Dickens Avenue is the new home of Jack Corbett, private first class, U.S. Marine Corps, serial number 2321157, blood type O, the great adventurer with serious second thoughts about the pending adventure that is unfolding before his eyes in this valley.

Pay

My military pay in Vietnam is in a currency called military payment certificates (MPC). My monthly pay rate for rank of private first class is $129. Added to that is about another $60 for being overseas in a combat zone. I haven't experienced any combat yet, except for being on the wrong end of a couple of rockets in Da Nang, so I consider that extra $60 to be gravy money.

Drawing pay at Khe Sanh, in the mountain highlands, away from civilization, is like a bad joke. There is no place to spend money except at the PX. How much toothpaste do you need? You can buy a candy bar, but the tropical heat has melted the chocolate inside the wrapper long before you open it. Because there are limited items to purchase, I have opted to have a portion of my pay withheld and invested in U.S. savings bonds on every scheduled pay date. I haven't done this out of patriotism. One day, if I am lucky, I will get home to America, and on that day I don't want to be broke. Looking forward to that day isn't easy, because I am not certain how much of a future I have left.

I have spent some money from my first pay and purchased two Kodak mailers, which are packages containing a roll of new film and an envelope for exposed film so I can return it to the company for processing. Postage and processing are paid upon purchase of these mailers. The envelope is pre-addressed to the Kodak Company in Rochester, New York. After developing the film, the company forwards the pictures to whatever return address you specify. I thought this was a wonderful way of doing business, so I purchased two Kodak mailers and I don't even have a camera. I am optimistic that I will find a camera somewhere.

Pastimes

During the calm before the expected storm here at Khe Sanh, late in the afternoons we are issued beer, Carling Black Label, when it is available. The beer might have been cold upon delivery, but by the time it is passed around it is warm. Who cares? Warm beer is better than no beer. Sometimes, when another Marine isn't up to drinking his ration, he barters his beer for cigarettes.

The afternoon beer issue provides us time to get together in small groups and shoot the breeze. We voice our opinions on whether or not—and if so, when—the North Vietnamese will attack. We are getting to know one another and finding out where each one of us is from back in the States.

I am adjusting to my new home and starting to make friends. Mark, from a small Virginia town called Stacey, is soft spoken; his kindness shows through his tough Marine exterior. I wonder how he, who never has a bad word to say, ended up in the Marines. He has been in Vietnam for nearly a year and has only three months remaining of his thirteen-month combat tour. When that is complete, he will be rotated back to the United States.

I have also made friends with Charles McIntyre. He doesn't like his given name. In fact, he prefers to be called any name but Charles. I can call him Mack, Mike, or even C.M. Mack is on his third thirteen-month combat tour in Vietnam. I wonder why anyone would want to stay in Vietnam for five minutes more than is required.

Mark is a squad leader of one of our mortar crews. Mack is a forward observer (FO). He has the job of venturing out beyond the combat base boundaries into enemy territory to locate targets for mortars and artillery placed here on the base. More times than not, he finds a target for our 81mm mortars to fire at.

Mack is half of a two-man team. The other half is his radio operator, Ben, a tall, muscular African American. Their bond from working together in enemy territory carries over to inside the base, when they are not on patrol. They are inseparable. Forward observers and their radio operators have mettle. They get up close, face-to-face with the enemy. They must hope that while they are looking at enemy faces, the enemy troops don't see their faces. They must keep their cool. I don't possess their skills or their courage.

Mack, from Norman, Oklahoma, acquired a girlfriend during his last thirty-day leave from Vietnam. A thirty-day furlough is granted to a Marine who has signed up for another tour of combat. You may take the leave upon finishing a thirteen-month tour, before you start your new one. Mack talks about his girlfriend, Patty, all the time.

I don't know if Mark from Virginia has a girlfriend. If he does, he has never mentioned her. Perhaps the long months he has endured in Vietnam have made girlfriends a sensitive topic.

More Intelligence

The rumors are now confirmed, and I don't like what I hear. One of the massing enemy units is the same unit that participated in the overthrow of the French outpost at Dien Bien Phu, during the French-Indochina war in Vietnam's battle with French troops on her soil in the 1950s. At Dien Bien Phu, the French were surrounded, laid siege to, then defeated. This battle ended French involvement in Vietnam. Current rumor has it that the enemy's intention is to make our combat base, Khe Sanh, America's Dien Bien Phu.

The rumor angers the Marines here. As new and combat inexperienced as I am, I know that there is no way any of us will allow our outpost to be taken by the enemy. If the enemy do manage to overrun us, it will be over our dead bodies.

I think the military strategists have decided to use us as bait. I think we are here to attract the enemy.

Enemy Types

The enemy in Vietnam have different faces. One face is the Viet Cong, the guerrillas. Some Viet Cong work in their farm fields and rice paddies during the day. At night they join their units to fight in the territories around their hamlets. The Viet Cong rely on the peasant population for support in the form of food, shelter, and secrecy regarding their identities and whereabouts. The Viet Cong also receive logistical support in the form of weapons, munitions, and medical supplies both trucked and hand carried to them via the Ho Chi Minh Trail. They are proficient fighters who improvise with what is at hand. Vietnam's rice paddies and jungle paths are their own backyard. They know the shortcuts, hidden trails, and watering holes; they know where to seek medical aid, where in the landscape to spring an ambush for a tactical advantage, when to disengage, in what direction to disperse, where to sleep, and where to assemble once again. It is guerrilla warfare in its purest form. Among the local peasant population are poppasans (men), mommasans (women), and babysans (children), all of whom would think nothing of hurling a grenade at you.

We are, to the Viet Cong and their sympathizers, the American imperialist aggressor meddling in their political affairs. There are

on some desolate beach along the New Jersey shore. The walls of the tower are filled with sandbags stacked one atop the other to a height of about four feet above the wooden floor. The walls could hopefully stop a sniper's bullet from striking the lower half of my body. The window spaces above the sandbags are completely open except for rough-cut wooden beams that support a crude roof. Looking from the sentry box, I see patches of jungle grass that slope down and away from the southern perimeter of our outpost. I don't have to look far in the distance before the carpet of jungle grasses disappears into the darkness.

This is my first night assigned to sentry duty at a listening post. I have been led by another Marine down a trail in the darkness and shown the exact location of this LP. My guide observed by my shiny new flak jacket and jungle utilities that I am a newcomer to Vietnam. The Marine I am to relieve gives me some basic instructions. He tells me to shout a challenge to anyone I see approaching our lines. He makes it clear that there are no "friendlies" on patrol outside our lines tonight; therefore, anyone I spot will be an enemy. He tells me that in four hours I will be relieved by another sentry, who, upon approaching my post, will call out to me through the darkness that he is my relief and about to come up on my position. The soldier I am relieving also instructs me not to take my eyes off the area I am responsible for guarding. As he starts up the trail, he suddenly stops, about-faces, and calls back to me in the darkness. "Hey! By the way, last night's first watch found a booby-trapped hand grenade at this post. Stay awake. Watch your back. They're really out there." Then he adds: "And don't fucking fall asleep!" I feel like thanking him for all the good news. I have no intention of falling asleep. He must think I am a fool. How could anyone fall asleep after hearing the intelligence reports about the enemy maneuvering their troops in our vicinity?

Here I am, standing like a jerk in the darkness at, of all places, the DMZ. I am right on the enemy's doorstep. Somewhere out there in the darkness are divisions of the North Vietnamese Army. I can't see them and I can't hear them, but my sixth sense tells me they are here. They are just not ready to attack.

Time passes slowly, and I am just staring and staring into the grassy fields and beyond toward the jungle tree line in the distance. I am trying to fine-tune my night vision and see as I have never seen in the dark before. It is a black night and, though I am trying, I can't see a thing. I strain my ears to detect any noise that seems out of place, but all I hear is my own labored, anxious breathing. I am nervous and scared. I can hear my heart pulsating within my chest. I would like a cigarette to calm my nerves, but I can't take the chance of lighting one. The enemy could see the flicker of my match.

Thoughts about the six high-ranking enemy officers recently killed, while scouting the base perimeter, go through my mind. I am hoping that if the enemy do any more scouting, it won't be during my watch. I wonder what the enemy are thinking. They are probably lying out there in the grass in front of my post, having a good laugh about some stupid Marine exposed to them in a stupid-looking LP. I feel as though I am standing on a stage and enemy divisions are my audience. I wish another Marine were on guard with me; then maybe I wouldn't be having these thoughts. Out here I am afraid of my own shadow. Actually, I am lucky there is no moon tonight to make a shadow.

Omens

It is January 19 and there is trouble. A platoon of India Company of my regiment's 3d Battalion is out on patrol. The mission is to retrieve a field radio left in the jungle two days ago when a team leader and his radioman were ambushed and killed. The men in the platoon are searching for the missing radio in an area seven hundred meters southwest of Hill 881 North (881N). They have just been ambushed by what is estimated to be several hundred North Vietnamese soldiers. Heavily outnumbered, the platoon is attempting to break free of the ambush and withdraw. The men are radioing for assistance from our artillery.

January 20 Morning

India Company is returning with more men to meet the enemy again. They set out this morning at 0500, using heavy ground fog for concealment. But now, at 0900, the fog has lifted and exposed them to the enemy. The North Vietnamese see them and open fire, inflicting heavy casualties on India Company with automatic rifles. Twenty men are wounded before they can scramble to cover. The lieutenant in charge of the platoon is killed. A recon team, accompanying India on this patrol, runs directly into the enemy. Two members of the team are killed and five are seriously wounded.

January 20 Afternoon

The fighting hasn't stopped. A medical evacuation helicopter flying in to retrieve some of the patrol's casualties is shot down. An air strike is called. Jet aircraft are dropping five-hundred-pound bombs around the patrol's positions.

I hear the sounds of war. Ban Shee and other artillery pieces on the combat base open fire in support of India Company. They fire close by India Company and try to create a wall of exploding shrapnel to shield the exposed Marines from the NVA and also to push the enemy back from attacking India Company's positions. India communicates by radio that Ban Shee and the other guns are on target. I am close up and watching the howitzer. I have to shield my ears from the loud blasts of their gun barrel noises. The fire support from the air strikes and artillery helps. India Company is beginning to get the upper hand on the enemy. The men are, as is said in the Corps, beginning to "kick ass and take names."

A seemingly untimely order is issued to India Company: break contact and withdraw back to the hilltop encampment at Hill 881 South (881S). India Company is stunned by this order. They are, at the moment, winning this battle. They don't know the reason for the order. I do. Less than an hour ago, the reason walked up to our lines at the eastern end of our airstrip, the section of the perimeter that I think needs more men to guard it. The reason is a North Vietnamese Army officer, Lieutenant Tonc. He approached our lines waving a white flag of surrender in one hand and his brand new AK-47 rifle in the other. He surrendered because he is angry at the North Vietnamese Army; they passed him over for a promotion and gave it to someone else. Lieutanant La Than Tonc is, or was at least an hour ago, the commanding officer of the enemy's 14th Antiaircraft Company, 95C Regiment, 325th Division.

Lieutenant Tonc brought more than his weapon and white flag with him when he came through our lines. He brought some timely information. While being interrogated at the base headquarters, he revealed that the hill outpost of 881S, from which India Company left for battle this morning, is targeted for attack this evening.

The reason Colonel Lownds, the 26th Marines regimental commander, ordered India Company to disengage is based on what Tonc told our commanders. Colonel Lownds ordered India Company to fall back so it will not be caught away from and isolated from its established defenses on 881S.

5: A Million-Dollar Wound

The Sounds of War

India Company is breaking contact with the NVA. I have been ordered down to the airstrip's loading zone, where help is needed to remove the wounded from the medevac helicopters that are extracting India's casualties from the field. I will be a stretcher bearer and help carry India Company's wounded from the helicopters to our base aid station, called Charlie Med, for Charlie Company, 3d Medical Battalion. Charlie Med will try to stabilize the wounded so they can be evacuated to larger medical facilities in the rear.

The first helicopter is approaching fast. The pilot knows that time means everything to the wounded men he has rescued from the battleground on Hill 881N. As we wait for the helicopter to touch down, we are all aware of the urgency of the moment and the seriousness of it all. As soon as the chopper touches down, we enter and remove the wounded as quickly but as gently as possible. We place them on collapsible canvas stretchers. Some we are able to place on the flat platforms of motorized mules. We are driving or carrying the wounded on our stretchers to Charlie Med as fast as possible.

What I am seeing is not pretty. As I run up the helicopter ramp and go inside, I slip on the blood of wounded Marines. The corpsmen in the field did what they could for these men. Most of the wounded have been injected with morphine and appear to be in shock. They are drugged to the point of being unaware of their surroundings, although some are still in pain. The eyes of all are glazed from the combat they have just seen. Several soldiers in the chopper are covered with ponchos. Their faces are covered, too. These soldiers didn't survive their wounds.

I hear the sounds of war inside the helicopter. It is not the sound of rifle fire. It is men groaning in pain. Some casualties are on the threshold of death. I am learning to recognize a certain change in the color of a dying man's skin; it turns bluish gray moments before life leaves his body. I don't like this. I am feeling guilty. I feel guilty about my motive for coming to Vietnam, coming to a war to satisfy a meaningless quest for adventure. Many of the casualties I am looking at, both dead and wounded, have come to Vietnam for a noble cause, at least in their minds. They have come to fight and help other people be free. I feel as though I am not worthy to be in their suffering presence.

On my second stretcher-bearing trip to Charlie Med, I carry a Marine who has been shot by an NVA with an AK-47 rifle. The bullet lodged in the Marine's upper right leg. While carrying him toward the back of the helicopter, I almost drop my end of the stretcher because I slip on the blood-slick deck. Achieving sure footing on the tarmac, I and the Marine bearing the other end of the stretcher finally head off with our casualty in the direction of Charlie Med.

As I talk to the wounded Marine on our stretcher, I offer words of encouragement and try to put him at ease. "We'll have you to Charlie Med in no time. Don't worry, you're gonna be okay," I shout at him. I want to make sure he hears me over the engine noises of the arriving and departing medevac helicopters. I yell any words of encouragement that come to mind. I know that if I had been shot and put on this stretcher, I would appreciate any inspiring words from anyone, the more people the better.

We carry our casualty, on the run, about half the distance to Charlie Med. My arms are tired, I am winded, and I'm looking at the wounded Marine. I suddenly realize that he is laughing. That angers me. What is so funny? I am physically exhausted and carrying this laughing Marine. "What the fuck are you laughing about? You've just been shot! Are you crazy?" He is looking at me now with a big grin on his face. "It's the million-dollar wound. I'm finally getting out of this fucking country and going home. I'm going home alive."

I am stunned by what he has just said. He is happy that he's been shot. He is going home, and I just got here. Maybe he's right; I think this Marine with the bullet in his leg might just be right about Vietnam. So I make a wish. I wish that I will be as lucky as he is. I hope that if I must get shot, it will be a million-dollar wound, just serious enough to get me home. I am learning fast.

Thanks to the information that Lieutenant Tonc revealed during his interrogation, our outpost is now on red alert, the highest state of readiness. It is believed that an attack on our post is likely. The discontented enemy officer revealed that the NVA is poised to strike.

Darkness, January 20 Evening to January 21 Early Morning

We have been at our gun pit since sundown and have prepared many high-explosive mortar rounds, which we have at the ready. We stare into the darkness of the perimeter, waiting for the enemy to attack, but nothing has happened yet. I am tired; my stretcher duty has taken its toll and I am anxiously awaiting the order to stand down.

Several of us are granted permission to get some sleep. In several hours we will return to relieve those who remain here on the guns. I retire to the hootch, which contains cots on the floor and stretchers suspended from the ceiling.

We have a full hootch tonight. My stretcher is vacant and awaiting me. The other three places to sleep are occupied. The Marines sleeping here are all members of my squad. There is tension in the air and in this hootch; I can feel it.

I lie awake on my stretcher. I am tired but I can't sleep. I have slept on this stretcher every night since my arrival at Khe Sanh nearly three weeks ago. Lying here and staring at the parachute that lines the ceiling of the hootch, I think about the Marine with the million-dollar wound. He was on the same type of stretcher that I am lying on now. I wonder how he is feeling and whether Charlie Med removed the bullets from his leg.

The only light in the underground hootch is provided by a small candle in an empty C-ration can. The candle and its holder rest on an empty wooden ammo box that serves as a table; it is positioned at the base of the sandbag steps leading down into the hootch. I have placed my glasses on the table next to the candle. I don't want to keep them in my rack with me, because I might roll on them in my sleep and break the frames.

A rat scratches the parachute ceiling liner. He is between the parachute silk and the fortifying materials of our roof. I can follow his itinerary by watching the moving, sagging bulges in the silk. Right now the rat is directly above my face. I have never seen rats as big as those here in Khe Sanh. I am not a rodent lover.

The other Marines in the bunker have fallen asleep one at a time. They are all sleeping now and there is a chorus of snoring.

0500

I still can't go to sleep. There is something else besides the rat keeping me awake now: loud and unfamiliar noises. The adventure I was seeking when I enlisted in the Marines is just beginning.

"Incoming! Incoming! On the guns!"

The sleeping Marines are now shouting and scrambling from our hootch and running to man the mortar. I hear loud explosions. Enemy rockets, artillery, and mortars are blasting into our base. The last Marine to run up the sandbag steps and exit the hootch accidentally knocks over the ammo box table; the candle topples to the floor and is extinguished. My glasses have been knocked somewhere onto the dirt floor and I can't find them in the dark. Without my glasses, my vision is poor. This is not the way to go to war.

Off to War

It is early in the morning on January 21, and sounds of exploding enemy shells become louder, indicating that they are impacting close to our positions at the eastern end of the combat base. Several sound as if they have exploded on the ground just outside. I need to make a decision. If I stay in the hooch and it takes a direct hit, I don't stand a chance. Even if I survive the hit, I will be buried alive from the collapse of dirt-filled sandbags and ammo boxes that make up our roof. I must make it to my foxhole, West Dickens Avenue, which is a smaller target. We dug those foxholes for an event such as this. It is time to go. My foxhole is about seventy-five yards from the hooch, in the direction of the airstrip. I will run for it and hope I don't get hit with shrapnel from an incoming enemy shell, but I will be running in the dark without my glasses. My eyes haven't had time to adjust to the darkness. I wish the candle in our bunker hadn't been lit in the first place. I am learning quickly that little mistakes have grave consequences. My error of looking at the lighted candle affected my night vision, so now I am at a serious disadvantage.

The dirt floor of the hooch is seven feet below the ground. As I feel my way in the darkness, my hands scrape the sculptured red clay walls of the entranceway. I blindly navigate the sandbag staircase, step-by-step. With each step the exploding shells striking the base become louder and louder, no longer muffled by the fortification materials of the hooch. The noise from the enemy rockets screaming in is new to me, and it is frightening.

I have made it outside the hooch and start walking in a half crouch in the general direction of where I think my foxhole is located. My ears ring from the explosions, and pieces of shrapnel make hissing and humming noises as they fly through the air around me. I am in danger and disorientated.

To lessen my chances of being hit, I crawl along the ground. I have covered only about half the distance to where I think my foxhole is when I decide to crawl into the first gun pit, trench line, foxhole, or depression in the ground I find. Flashes of fire from incoming explosions are visible one moment, then immediately gone. Their brief, sharp light prevents my eyes from adjusting to the darkness. What little flashes of light the explosions do give off, if only for a fraction of a second, don't help me spot a place to hide.

I no longer know where I am going, and I stop crawling. I am desperate, lying on the ground and wishing I could claw deep into the soil and hide. I am trying to stay calm and not panic, but here, above ground, I can easily get wounded. I don't believe the predicament I'm in. Everyone else made it to his foxhole.

In the darkness I hear someone shouting in my direction. I recognize the voice of our gunner, Bill. "It's me, Corbett," I shout back, hoping he can hear me above the noise.

"What the fuck are you doing lying out there on the ground?" he asks.

"My night vision is gone. My glasses are somewhere on the floor of the hooch. I can't see where the fuck I'm going. I can't even see you."

Bill shouts back. "Listen to me yell and follow the sound of my voice."

Frantically crawling in that direction, I reach the gun pit. Hands from inside the pit reach over the waist-high sandbags and unceremoniously hoist me over the top, then drop me on the deck.

My mortar squad is blindly firing round after round of 81mm high explosives, hoping to strike one of the NVA guns that is firing at us. The gun pit glows for a split second each time a round is fired from the barrel. Each mortar round dropped down the barrel strikes the firing pin, and its black-powder charges ignite and send the bomb on its way. The noise is harsh to my ears. My squad leader, dismayed, realizes I won't be of much help, even to fetch ammo, without my glasses.

"I'll go find your glasses. Just give me an idea where they are." I tell him, and he runs toward the hooch.

I have never been shelled before. Incoming enemy fire makes various noises as it comes in over our heads. Some rounds screech; some hiss wildly as they fly through the air. Based on the different sounds, I can tell we are being fired on by several types of weapons. Bombs explode differently, and some explosions are louder than others, but all can kill a person who is too close. Bill returns. Using a flashlight, he has found my glasses in the hooch. He hands them to me and tells me I am not needed to run ammo because there is ammunition remaining in the bunker attached to the gun pit. He tells me to go to my foxhole and take cover, which is fine with me. I can see now.

I probably set a record covering the distance between our gun pit and my foxhole. Jumping in, I realize that staying in the un-roofed part of my fighting hole, the front section facing the perimeter, wouldn't be too smart, because lots of shrapnel is whizzing through the air. Pieces of it could zing into my foxhole and wound me; worse, I could be killed.

I crawl through the passageway and into the back section, roofed with sandbags and dirt-filled ammo boxes. I find two Marines huddled inside. What are they doing in my foxhole? This is *my* refuge. I dug it. I tell them they can stay, but they better make room for me. Both Marines are in shock from the pandemonium around us. As each moves to one side, I crawl in and squeeze between them. From where I am sitting, I can see the open part of my fighting hole through the passageway. Though I am under my sandbagged roof, I am not as protected as my two guests. If a round strikes the front of the hole, the shrapnel could explode down the open passageway and strike me.

We are shoulder to shoulder and can't fully sit up; I should have dug the back section a little deeper. At first there is no conversation, but after a while we share remarks, shouting to one another to be heard above the explosions. Enemy shells that strike close by shake the ground and cause loosened dirt from the sandbags on my roof to pour down on our heads and shoulders. Perhaps I should have put more sandbags and ammo boxes on top of the roof, as other Marines did. Perhaps I shouldn't have been so lazy. It's a little late now.

The Ammunition Dump

We have been holed up in here for nearly an hour. There is no letup in the number of explosions. Enemy incoming has struck the base ammunition dump with rockets. The dump is not far from our mortar emplacements, and its stores of ammunition are igniting and blowing up over our positions. We are going to be in this hole while the dump explodes. It is too dangerous to get out. It sounds as though all the Fourth of July fireworks of my youth have come back to blow up, altogether, this morning. The constant noise of many explosions starts to disorientate us. The three of us discuss fleeing my fighting hole and getting farther away from the exploding ammo dump, but the idea is quickly rejected because we can't chance, however briefly, exposing ourselves on open ground.

The horrendous noise hurts our eardrums so badly that in desperation we tear the filters off cigarettes and plug them into our ears to muffle the sound. It helps. We smoke cigarettes one after another, even the ones we made filterless. Dirt continues to spill down on us from shaken sandbags on the roof. Our situation is worsening. What could possibly happen next?

Someone screams, "Gas!" The canisters of tear gas stored in our ammo dump are blowing up, and I don't have my gas mask. The gas cloud is drifting over our eastern perimeter and has engulfed West Dickens. Its fumes reach us, coming up the passageway and into the back of my foxhole. My eyes are watering and my mucous membranes are irritated. I grab my poncho liner—a light, downy blanket—and cover my face, hoping that the liner will filter some gas fumes and help me breath better. Only one of us has a mask. I offer the other maskless Marine one end of my poncho liner to hold against his face.

There is not enough space back here. Three of us are squeezed inside a hole that is big enough for only one, and it is making me claustrophobic. The North Vietnamese are pouring it on. They are firing rockets, artillery, and mortars into our outpost. Their 122mm rockets weigh 125 pounds each and are 9 feet long. If one hits West Dickens, I know that the roof I made won't stop it.

Ammo Man

"Corbett, we need ammo!" My name is being called. Now, of all times, my gun squad needs mortar rounds. All the mortar rounds in our gun pit's ammunition bunker have been fired at the enemy.

We have another bunker with a couple of hundred mortar rounds inside it; the bunker is about twenty-five yards from the gun pit. I crawl out the passageway to the front of the foxhole and look around. Smoke shrouds our emplacements, and some fires are burning. Pieces of shrapnel, large and small, all potentially lethal, zing through the air around me. The shrapnel from enemy incoming is mixed with the shrapnel from our exploding dump. The ground around my foxhole is littered with hundreds of tiny steel arrows that come from the beehive artillery ordnance stored in our ammo dump. Beehive is the nickname for flechette artillery rounds, which contain thousands of miniature steel arrows. Some steel arrows have impaled the sandbags of my foxhole.

I have seen enough. It's time to find out what I'm made of. Leaving the relative safety of West Dickens to run ammo goes against my instinct for self-preservation, so I hesitate. I prod myself with the thought that I am a Marine with a job to perform and that is why I'm here. My squad needs ammo immediately, and I'm going to get it.

As I run back and forth between the ammo bunker and our gun pit, pieces of shrapnel wing by. The larger pieces and the ones with greater velocity make the most noise as they cut through the air. I am terrified as I run one box of ammunition at a time. Each of the boxes contains three mortar rounds. When I reach the gun pit, I push the box over the top of the sandbags to another Marine in the gun pit. He unpacks the rounds and rips off the correct number of black-powder bags from the bomb's fin assembly, ensuring that the mortar projectile will fire the desired distance from our gun to the target.

With each new run for ammunition, I expect to get wounded. The bunker that I am fetching the rounds from is on fire, but I determine that it is still safe to enter. The flames are on the bunker's outside walls and roof, but all that is burning is the cloth material of the sandbags. At the moment, there is no danger to the ammo inside the bunker. At the gun pit, the situation is grave. It is too dangerous for the squad.

An NVA 82mm mortar round is on target, but it doesn't explode. The round is punched into the ground only feet from our gun pit. If it had exploded, some of us would have been wounded, or worse.

Because of the many rounds our mortar is firing, its barrel is hot and glowing, and there is danger that the hot barrel could prematurely ignite the cloth bags of black-powder propellant as a projectile is dropped down the barrel. We don't have any water handy to cool the barrel, so each of us, in turn, urinates on the gun to cool it down. It is easy for me to urinate, because until this moment it has been the furthest thing from my mind, and there has been no time.

We fire our mortar rounds into the surrounding terrain using coordinates that we have preregistered and written down. We are one of the few guns on the combat base still firing back. Everyone else has taken shelter from enemy shells. It is hard to believe that we are standing in this gun pit under enemy fire, shooting at targets we can't see.

Even with our base's main ammunition dump exploding, with fires burning all around us, with our mortar's barrel still glowing and overheating, with an unexploded enemy mortar round sticking out of the dirt several feet away, the men in my squad are singing. Though I am undoubtedly the most scared Marine in Khe Sanh at the moment, I am also the proudest because of the song we are singing: the "Marine Corp Hymn." "From the halls of Montezuma to the shores of Tripoli, we will fight our country's battles on land or on the sea." I join in. This singing together, under these circumstances, keeps our courage up. I am very proud to be here with these Marines.

Lieutenant Tonc, the enemy soldier who surrendered yesterday afternoon, was not lying. Our men on Hill 861 were attacked before midnight. The Marines up there were in hand-to-hand combat, and their hilltop took fire from enemy rockets and mortars. The North Vietnamese were in the Marine trench lines. Their captain was wounded three times in several hours and their gunny sergeant was killed. The 81mm mortar crews on their hilltop fired off nearly seven hundred rounds at the attacking NVA soldiers. Hill 861's mortar squads did what I hope I will never have to do: They fired their mortar nearly straight up so the rounds would fall back and explode right in front of their own positions. The Marines up there held their ground.

It is believed that the enemy rockets being fired into our base's ammo dump come from Hill 881N. Our ammo dump continues to blow up in explosions of varying sizes, depending on the amount of ammunition cooking off in the fires. The lesser explosions tell me that a few boxes just blew up. The larger blasts tell me that a full pallet or two of ammo has blown up. Each blast is spectacular and frightening to watch and illuminates our positions in the predawn darkness. I am sure the explosions can be seen by the Marines on the hilltop positions. From our mortar emplacements we have the most spectacular view because Khe Sanh's ammunition dump is our neighbor.

As stocks of mortar rounds are nearly depleted, our final targets are enemy positions around the old Khe Sanh village. As with Hill 861, Marines there, positioned with the village militia, are also under attack from the North Vietnamese infantry. They have radioed a request for reinforcements from our base. Although enemy troops have already penetrated their compound, their request is denied by our commander because he anticipates a ground attack by the NVA on our outpost. We fire for the Marines at Khe Sanh village with our mortar. We drop the bombs where they tell us. We use our remaining ammo in an attempt to help them. Hopefully, the Marines in the village can hold. When we are out of mortar rounds, an order is given from our fire directional center, via our radio headset: "Stand down. Take cover!" It's about time. Our mortars have been returning fire since the attack first started. I believe that we are the last to leave our guns.

I run back to my foxhole, leap in, and crawl into the passageway to enter the sheltered section, but I stop. I suddenly remember the claustrophobic feeling I experienced while back there earlier this morning. I didn't like the feeling of not being able to move about. I didn't like the fear I experienced while waiting for the unseen and unexpected to happen. I decide to remain in the open part. Here, at least,

I can see what is going on and not be wondering about it. If things become too dangerous, I still have the option of taking refuge in the back, but I hope things don't get any worse than they already are.

I prepare myself for the worst possible scenario, the one that Lieutenant Tonc told to my superior officers during his interrogation: a ground assault by the enemy. This is the sector of our defenses where Lieutenant Tonc said they would attack: right here, in full view of my foxhole. Why not? Lieutenant Tonc walked up to this side of the perimeter.

I check my M16 automatic rifle and put all my available magazines within easy reach. I have several magazines, with eighteen rounds in each, instead of the twenty bullets the ammo clips can hold. This keeps excessive tension off the spring inside the magazine and ensures that the spring pushes out the bullets. All my hand grenades are within easy reach, too. Sitting in my foxhole, I am hyperalert. Periodically I look out toward our defensive lines; I raise my head just enough to see over the sandbags. I scan the immediate area and look for any signs of alarm from nearby Marines, which would signal the approach of enemy troops.

My West Dickens Avenue sign has toppled over. While awaiting a possible assault from enemy ground troops, a thought enters my mind that puts me at ease: If I can't leave my foxhole and move safely about this area because of flying shrapnel, then neither can the enemy.

I calm down and settle into a pattern. Whenever I hear an exceptionally loud blast, I curl into a fetal position, pull my helmet snugly on my head, grab my balls to protect them with one hand, and shield my face with my other hand. I am adapting to the enemy incoming and our exploding ammo dump. When there is a lull in the number of explosions, I inch my way up and scan the perimeter again.

During my quick look-sees, I determine that the base's main ammunition dump continues to roar, explode, burn menacingly, and blast debris over our positions. Located to the left of West Dickens, the ammo dump litters my foxhole with fragments of hot shrapnel.

Some pieces of shrapnel, their velocity expended, hit the ground gently. Other fragments hiss loudly as they whiz over our heads, still at deadly speed, their momentum not diminished.

Sunrise

The first light of day this morning is barely distinguishable from the glow of the burning dump. Though I am facing east, I can't see the rising sun through the smoke coming from the many fires in our sector. I hear the muffled engine of a spotter plane circling just above us. The sound gives me unexpected comfort; at least someone knows that our outposts have been attacked. I keep my body as low as I can in my foxhole and in a position that provides the smallest possible target for shrapnel. In addition to shrapnel, the ammo dump is blowing up and raining down unexploded ordnance; live mortar and artillery shells lay scattered on the ground around us. The ammo dump is an inferno. The fire will have to blow itself out, literally. I wonder about casualties. Who has been wounded? Who is dead?

As the sun rises higher, the visibility improves. I wonder how long I will be forced by the exploding ammo to remain in this hole. There are no charging NVA yet. I look toward other foxholes but don't see any faces. Everyone is holed up, taking cover, keeping his head down.

I wonder how much of the twelve hundred tons of ammunition and fuel stored in the dump is left to blow up. My answer comes with a spectacular explosion accompanied by a reddish-orange fireball. Whatever ammo remained in the dump has ignited in unison. Tremendous shock waves roll out from the center of the blast and ripple in all directions. They are coming toward me. The noise of the explosion hurts my ears. I need to protect myself. The shock waves will be over me in a split second. I lay down in my foxhole on my stomach, instinctively grasp my balls with one hand, cover my face with my other hand, and hope for the best.

The shock waves reach me. The sensation is like nothing I have ever felt before. The concussion thrusts me out of my foxhole and into the air. My body is suspended for a second above the ground.

Then the shock waves slam my body back down into my foxhole. I land hard, on my back, and it hurts. The noise is so loud that it must be heard in Saigon, several hundred miles away.

On my back, I am looking straight up and seeing sky. For a moment I am stunned and in shock. I try to regain my senses. I look straight up as a huge cloud of debris, blown up in the massive explosion, climbs into the sky above me. It seems to be happening in slow motion. There is a loud hissing sound as the rubble begins its fall back to the ground. I am in danger of being struck by the falling debris. I crawl under the covered passageway of my foxhole. As I crawl, I feel tremendous pain in my back from being slammed into my hole. There is no time to make it to the back of the hole; the passageway, roofed with sandbags, must do. This is madness.

I look toward the unroofed section of my foxhole. I see scorched, unexploded mortar rounds raining down from the sky. A brass artillery casing from the ammo dump rockets into my foxhole and ricochets off the dirt side wall, gouging a large chunk of soil from its hardened, weathered surface. The casing impacts with such tremendous velocity that, had I stayed up front, it would have taken my head off. More debris fills the front of my foxhole. Whatever stored explosives remained are now being blown up and out of the dump. Debris covers the ground around our positions. It falls into the nearby trenches and fighting holes.

I hope with this last tremendous explosion that the worst is over. It now might be safer to exit West Dickens, look around, and assess the situation. I no longer hear the whistling of incoming enemy rounds. I don't know exactly when the enemy stopped shelling us. The noise from the ammo dump has been so loud, it has dominated all other sounds.

There is work to do before leaving my foxhole. One round at a time, I carefully remove unexploded ordnance from the front of my hole. Gingerly, I lift each round up and out and place it off to the side of my foxhole. I will keep the large brass artillery casing that could have taken my head off and use it for both a conversation piece and an ashtray.

Later, I check on my fellow Marines nearby. The ones I see in their foxholes are visibly dazed. Nobody is talking. The trauma of the last several hours has taken its toll on all of us. At our end of the perimeter, miraculously, our casualties are few. Our trench lines and foxholes have done their jobs. All our digging has paid off.

We take a head count. Several Marines are suffering from shrapnel wounds; some of the wounded manage to bandage themselves. We tend to and carry the more seriously wounded to our battalion aid station, Charlie Med. There will be fewer familiar faces now. There is still smoke and fires. Thousands of pieces of shrapnel carpet the ground, and hundreds of charred live explosive rounds are scattered about the area, but at least I'm still alive.

January 21, 1968, Late Morning

We must replenish our stocks of mortar rounds. My mortar squad commandeers a mechanical mule to make ammunition runs, and we have located pallets of mortar rounds at our airstrip's loading zone. The ammo dump continues to blow up periodically, but none of the explosions is as large as this morning's.

We gather the unexploded ordnance that litters the ground and put it into piles. As a result there are mounds of rubble everywhere I look, but now it will be safer to walk around our sector. We inspect our fortifications and see they have held up well. On some sandbags, where the fabric casing was burned away, the heated dirt inside remains molded in place, like a large brick just out of a kiln.

The enemy guns are firing at us again; coming through the air is the now familiar mix of rockets, artillery, and mortar rounds. As I listen to the new incoming slam our outpost, I realize that this battle isn't over; it is just beginning.

We return fire with our new stocks of ammunition, firing blindly at unlocated enemy emplacements. Their artillery and rocket emplacements are out of our mortar's range, so we can only hope to strike enemy troops or one of their mortars. It is logical that their 82mm mortar must be in range of our 81mm mortar, because it is basically the same weapon with the same range.

We fire high-explosive rounds that blast out shrapnel on impact, and also white phosphorus rounds. Our forward observers haven't yet been able to pinpoint any of the enemy guns, though we can hear them when they fire at us.

While assisting with our mortar's fire missions, I see some tiny steel darts sticking out from my clothing. The darts are from the flechette rounds that exploded from the ammo dump earlier this morning. I am fortunate that the arrows have penetrated only my clothing and not my skin. My once shining jungle utilities shine no more. My clothes are torn and dirt stained and even have some burn marks, a consequence of my early-morning runs to our flaming ammo bunker. My shirt has a few blood spots from minor cuts and scratches. I guess I am not the "fucking new guy" anymore.

With the destruction of our main ammo dump, the base has lost the bulk of its ammunition. The appearance of the base as I have known it for the last three weeks has also changed. Our company mess hall has been blown up. The nearby tent with the raised sides and waist-high sandbag walls has been reduced to ashes, and only scorched sandbags outline the rectangular section of ground where the tent once was. Many of our water-filled canvas bags suspended on a tripod no longer contain water; they are riddled with shrapnel holes. Our makeshift shower is in splinters. The steel matting surface on the airstrip is pocked with craters where enemy rockets and artillery struck and exploded. The tarmac needs immediate repairs. We have serious damage to our infrastructure.

From this day on, everything we eat will be from cans. I will have to fetch for myself all the water I drink. All our provisions will have to be replenished by either helicopters or airplanes. No supply trucks dare come up the jungle road, Route 9, from Dong Ha. Whatever few amenities existed on this base before this morning will have no priority over ammo, food, and medical supplies. Creature comforts will become scarce or cease to exist. We will still receive mail; letters don't weigh much or take up much cargo space on aircraft. Our mail is our morale.

On my first day under enemy fire, I have learned important lessons. My hearing is now attuned to the sounds (muzzle blasts)

Vietnamese peasants who can set up a boobytrap (rigged explosive) with the skill and cunning of a professional soldier and with the same deadly consequences. These are the same Vietnamese civilians, we have been told, whom we are here to help defend against Communist military aggression from people of their own nationality in North Vietnam. We are fighting for the South Vietnamese people's right to democratically determine their own political destiny.

Our enemy in the vicinity of Khe Sanh are different from the Viet Cong. We are up against the regular North Vietnamese Army (NVA), which is well fed, well armed, well uniformed, and highly disciplined. The men have all the weapons necessary for waging war. Their arsenal includes tanks, artillery, rocket launchers, mortars, automatic weapons, and field radios to coordinate the use of these weapons. The men wear web belts or red leather belts with chrome buckles with the insignia of a Communist star on the buckle in bas-relief.

Intelligence continues to accumulate. Returning Marine patrols confirm that the enemy have surrounded us in huge numbers. All indications are that they are about to knock on our door.

Listening Post

Tonight I am assigned to man one of our listening posts (LPs). These are located at the extreme edges of our defensive perimeter, just outside our lines, beyond the strands of barbed and razor wire that encircle the perimeter of the entire combat base. The LPs are positioned at set intervals along the length of our boundaries. Some LPs are similar to prison guard towers in that they are places from which we can observe the surrounding ground. But unlike prison towers, our LPs are for the purpose of keeping people out, not in. Anyone manning an LP should see the enemy first. An LP is not always a fixed structure that one can observe from. The term can also apply to a randomly chosen piece of ground.

The listening post I am guarding is a small tower several feet higher than the surrounding grade. My LP is weathered and looks like a poorly constructed lifeguard stand, such as one you might see made as enemy artillery is fired. I have learned that there are usually several seconds between the time I hear the enemy guns fire and the time the round itself actually strikes. That is important, because it gives me a few seconds to run and jump into a foxhole or a trench for cover. Those few precious seconds could save my life.

January 21 Sundown

I am back at West Dickens and reerecting my street sign, which was blown over by the concussion from the ammo dump. I prepare for my first night of living in my foxhole, because I won't be sleeping in the hooch anymore; it is too dangerous. The only thing it is good for now is storage. I get a blanket and ready my field jacket, preparing for the cold night. I wonder what it will be like to sleep in the open part of my foxhole on the Khe Sanh perimeter. Will I be able to sleep when I know that the enemy could come charging up through the grass just yards away?

I am caught up in the sequence of events here at Khe Sanh. Three weeks ago I had never heard of the place; I couldn't even pronounce the name. I use what daylight remains to write my first letter home. My parents have no idea where I am in Vietnam, nor do they know which Marine outfit I am assigned to. I don't want them to worry, so I lie in the letter. I write that I am with a Marine detachment in Saigon. I exaggerate and say that I have the opportunity, on weekends, to play a round of golf. I have written a bunch of lies. If I am wounded or killed here, they will find out soon enough, so it is needless for them to know where I really am. My lies will hopefully keep them from worrying, and I won't have to worry about them worrying about me. I have enough things to worry about here.

Last Call

I am angry because it just occurred to me that, due to the enemy shelling of our outpost, we have missed our afternoon beer ration. I am angry at the North Vietnamese. The bastards!

Each mortar squad is responsible for assigning a man to radio watch in the gun pit. Someone must be on watch during the night while others sleep. The Marine on watch wears radio headphones that are connected by communication wire (called a land line) that runs on top of the ground and connects to the fire directional center (FDC). The soldier on watch waits for radio transmissions from the FDC and listens for one command in particular: "Guns up, fire mission, on the guns!" If he hears this command through his earphones, it is his responsibility to alert those who are sleeping. We divide the night watches equally, usually two hours each. Each man takes a watch.

It is nightfall once again. There were moments this morning when I didn't think I would live to see this night. I am assigned the first radio watch of the evening, and I wear the headphones and listen for any transmission from the FDC. I haven't heard anything yet. The earphones are tight and uncomfortable; they are so snug that they prevent me from hearing any other sounds. My ears are attuned to the FDC only. I have already decided I don't like radio watches, because if the enemy fire their guns, I won't be able to hear them and I won't know there is incoming in the air and on the way. Wearing these headphones is robbing me of those precious seconds that are needed to jump into a foxhole.

After Watch

My watch is over. I return to my hole and prepare for sleep. It is cold tonight, so I put on my field jacket and spread my rain poncho on the dirt floor. Before sleeping I ready my weapons: hand grenades, M16, ammo clips, and bayonet. Then I curl into a fetal position. I wear my combat helmet when I sleep. I remove my glasses and place them at arm's length; I close my eyes and practice retrieving my glasses in the dark. If the enemy attack, my glasses will be the first thing I need; I won't have time to fumble around looking for them. I seek the most comfortable position for falling asleep. For added warmth, I cover myself with my poncho liner. I am exhausted. It has been a long, long day.

I haven't slept more than twenty minutes when I hear rockets and artillery shells being fired into the outpost. Several strike nearby. Shrapnel strikes some wires attached to the trip flares in our defensive barbed wire and the flares ignite, each heralded by a loud "POP." I extend my arm, retrieve my glasses, and rise to look out of my hole. I scan our perimeter, but all I see is the brilliant light from our perimeter trip flares. I look to the sides of the flares for the enemy. I watch until the flares burn out. I see no enemy soldiers.

I lie back down and try to go to sleep. I have learned another lesson: It is not easy to go to sleep when the same people who have been trying to kill me all day are still trying.

6: On the Job Training

Routines

It is the morning of January 22. Several bunkers were struck by enemy shells during the night and some Marines were killed. They can't enjoy the morning, as I can. Random incoming fire is taking us one by one, sometimes taking more than one.

At first light I look over our barbed wire defenses, because enemy troops may have infiltrated close to our lines under the cover of night. There are no enemy soldiers by our wire. I make instant coffee, which I do every morning. I won't leave my foxhole until I drink it.

Before the North Vietnamese attacked us, I would normally "shit, shower, and shave" right after coffee, but now that the shower has been blown up, I just sponge-bathe. Even if our shower were still there, I wouldn't use it. Who wants to stand in a shower naked when there is a possibility of being shelled?

After eating C rats for breakfast, or just coffee, we gather at our gun pit and talk about anyone we know who might have become a casualty during the previous night and whether or not he will be evacuated. It is a paradox. We don't want him to stay here, but we don't want to see him go.

We assign work details for the day and choose who will make ammunition and water runs. I draw a work detail every day, because I am still a newcomer. We will be making ammunition runs every day for a while, because our stock of mortar rounds is low. We have fired off only a few rounds on recent fire missions, because we are conserving our ammo. We fire just enough to strike at the enemy and let them know that we know where they are and would kill them if we had more ammunition. I don't mind ammunition runs, but I dislike water runs. The water is fetched and carried in five-gallon cans, and we each carry two cans. Carrying two water-filled cans even a short distance makes my arms feel as though they are being pulled from their sockets. The weight makes my fingers stay tightly curled around an imaginary handle even after my delivery is complete and I have put down the cans.

After we perform chores, we listen to Vietnam's armed forces radio station. The station broadcasts country and western music every morning for an hour. I have already learned that the country and western hour belongs to Roger, a Marine from Virginia. The fact that he is from Virginia might explain his taste in music. I don't like country and western music, because I am from New York and my radio, back stateside, was always tuned to rock and roll. Country and western music is depressing. If my woman left me, my horse or dog died, or I wrecked my pickup truck, I certainly would not sing about it. But Roger is a much meaner-looking Marine than I am, so I listen to country and western music each morning, all the while hoping that his radio batteries die.

During the morning get-together at the gun pit, I meet Ackerman. He is from Florida and is a devoted fan of a rock group named The Doors. When Roger is finished listening to country music, Ackerman plays rock music at full volume to get even with Roger. Roger doesn't like rock and roll. Ackerman is full of surprises. He has been in Vietnam for eight months, and shortly after his arrival he wrote to his congressman in Florida and requested a Florida state flag. The congressman obliged and mailed him a flag that is a clone of the one that waves over the Florida state capitol building in Tallahassee. It's big. When I first met Ackerman, he mentioned that he had the flag, but I hadn't seen it until now. He had kept it wrapped, saying he was saving it for a special occasion. At the moment, we are being shelled by the North Vietnamese. The timing of the morning shelling is so consistent that we have named it the "morning shelling"; it usually happens about ten o'clock. Ackerman has decided that this particular morning shelling is the special occasion he has been waiting for; he is going to wave his flag at the enemy. In the trench line, alongside Ackerman, I watch as he unwraps his huge flag. He unfurls it and waves it madly over his head. I think he is trying to signal the enemy gunners that they haven't yet hit him with a shell.

Incoming mortar and artillery shells strike closer and closer to our trench line. The North Vietnamese are using Ackerman's flag as a reference point. They are aiming at it. As explosions inch closer, I break into a cold sweat. Ackerman continues his enthusiastic flag waving. The enemy gunners must think they are firing at something of strategic importance, possibly a command bunker. Caught up in his flag-waving frenzy, Ackerman does not realize, as everyone else does, that he is aiding the enemy gunners. I haven't said a word to discourage him from his flag waving, but some other Marines, on the receiving end of the incoming, scream at me and Ackerman from their positions. They call Ackerman a "fucking maniac," among other things. Suddenly a Marine jumps out from a nearby foxhole, comes running, and rips the flag out of Ackerman's hands. Without breaking stride, he returns to his foxhole and jumps in, crumpling Ackerman's flag on his way. More enemy shells explode at ground level among our positions. None of us is wounded, no thanks to Ackerman. Then the North Vietnamese cease firing, probably believing they have blown up the flag and Ackerman along with it.

Immediately after the incident, Ackerman is ordered to report to the lieutenant in charge of our mortar section. Orders are being drawn up to transfer him out of Khe Sanh to a combined action company (CAP).

Spare Time

In my spare time between work details, ammunition and water runs, and fire missions on our mortar, I seek refuge and solitude in West Dickens. Sometimes I reach for my guitar and my Mel Bay self-instruction book. So far I have mastered the letter and note name of each of my six strings. I have learned where to position my fingers to play several rudimentary musical chords. Thanks to Mel Bay, I have graduated to singing and playing such difficult songs as "Home on the Range," "Merrily We Roll Along," "Carry Me Back to Old Virginia," "In the Evening in the Moonlight," and "Home, Home, How Can I Forget Thee." One song I found that causes objects to be thrown at my foxhole when I sing it is "The Caissons Go Rolling Along." I guess it's because caisson sounds too similar to Khe Sanh. I am in my own musical Stone Age.

My guitar playing, I have discovered, adds to the tension that already exists here. I discovered this when the E string of my instrument snapped and two nearby Marines cheered.

In my leisure moments I learn how to make an appealing meal of C rations. Some of the canned choices are beef and potatoes with gravy, pork slices, spaghetti and meatballs, ham and lima beans, ham and eggs, a canned biscuit, crackers and cheese, cookies, pound cake, and peanut butter. I opened and tasted the ham and eggs; never again. They look like discolored cream cheese and smell like skin cream. The ham and lima bean meal, though nutritious, makes me feel as though I am consuming watered down rat pellets. It is the most disliked choice of C rations in Vietnam. The soldiers call it "ham and motherfuckers." I will never open another can of them.

My nutritional needs are fulfilled from the other selections. My favorite meal is of my own creation. It is a reasonable facsimile of a grilled cheese sandwich. I use a small empty C-rat can for a stove and perforate the sides of the can with the tip of my bayonet so the heat tab, provided with the C rations, will get enough oxygen in the can to burn. I squeeze the rounded open end of the can until it is bent into an oval shape. This is to keep the biscuit that I am toasting atop the flame from falling into the can. When the biscuit is browned on both sides, I cut it in half, spread it with the cheese, and return it to the fire for a moment. It isn't bad.

The C-ration meals are accompanied by an accessory packet that contains instant coffee with powdered cream and sugar. The pack also contains plastic eating utensils, a chocolate bar, a finger towel, a minipack of toilet paper, a blue heat tab for cooking, a pack of gum containing two Chicklets, and a packet of four cigarettes. The brands are limited. Marlboro, the most popular brand, is a form of currency at Khe Sanh. I have the luck of the draw. In my accessory packs I have repeatedly received Marlboros. As my stock of them increases, so does my currency. I smoke unfiltered cigarettes, preferably Lucky Strike. Other Marines regularly give me their unfiltered cigarettes, hoping I will give them filtered ones in return.

The C rations I don't like I store in a wooden ammo box in the back of my fighting hole. Our stomachs become smaller, because food portions in C rations, though nutritionally ample, are small.

Although I adjust to the food, the water still causes me attacks of diarrhea. I am not yet immune to the water's parasites. Though I have halazone water purification tablets to sterilize the water in my canteen, I don't use them, because they give the water such a horrid flavor that I can't drink it. So it is either die of thirst or put up with diarrhea.

One attack of diarrhea almost costs me my life. While on the throne of the nearby outhouse, a rocket attack begins. Under two "attacks" then, I am determined to remain seated and finish my business. I look through the open door as the trench line that the outhouse faces fills up with Marines taking cover from the incoming fire. One by one their eyes fix on my eyes. They wonder when I am going to jump from the seat, pull up my trousers, and run for cover. I decide to take my chances. The Marines in the trench don't realize I have diarrhea.

A rocket whistles in and explodes on the ground between the trench line and my outhouse, blasting up a cloud of dirt. A large piece of shrapnel dings off the metal barrel that serves as the receptacle for the toilet on which I am perched. With this, the Marines in the trench line become an audience and I become the show. Suddenly, I hear their roars of laughter. I jump up, wipe myself as fast as I can, and run toward their trench line for shelter, my trousers still partway down. I run in short, choppy steps, trying to keep myself from tripping and falling to the ground. We are being attacked with rockets and the men are laughing.

As a result of the attack, the access road to Khe Sanh, Route 9, is now in enemy hands. All our needs will have to be supplied by helicopter, cargo plane, or parachute.

What's That?

On water detail once again, I fill my two jerry cans at the pumping station by the center of our outpost and start back to my mortar section at the eastern end of the outpost. "SHEEEEEEE." I hear the sound of an enemy rocket on its way. It sounds as though it is right above me and about to strike. I drop my water cans to the ground and frantically look for shelter. I don't see a foxhole or a trench that I can reach within the few seconds I have before the rocket strikes and explodes. I see ruts in the base road, made by truck tires, in what was once mud, but they are now dry and hardened. I dive inside a tire track to present the lowest possible profile to avoid shrapnel when the rocket strikes. I wait for the impact, but nothing explodes. It is not a rocket. I had heard the noise of a jet engine. The whispering sounds of an incoming rocket and a jet engine are similar. As I watch the jet, I see that it is at low altitude. It circles in the sky and flies east. It is flying low and slow, and the engines are sputtering. The plane and pilot must be in trouble. The plane has been struck by enemy antiaircraft fire and the pilot is ejecting. The pilot obviously wants to parachute down and land within the safety of our perimeter.

The pilot has blown off the jet canopy and has jettisoned. He is drifting to the ground strapped in his ejection seat. His parachute is gliding him out and over the eastern end of the perimeter. He descends slowly and disappears beyond our barbed wire defenses and over the sloping chasm of grass that tapers down from our lines into the valleys to the east. He could parachute right into enemy positions.

I abandon the water cans and run toward our mortar section. Several Marines off in the distance scramble for their weapons and quickly ready themselves to go outside our lines and attempt to rescue the pilot. A helicopter quickly rises from our airstrip. It is flying out over the perimeter several feet above the ground, its rotors loudly slapping the air just above our heads. It follows the pilot, who is still floating in his parachute silk, down into the valley.

The helicopter descends lower into the valley; it is gone for one long minute, then reappears. It retrieves the pilot. I watch his pilotless jet continue in flight after his ejection. The aircraft has rolled over on its back and nose-dived into the mountains to the east of Hill 1015.

The pilot is fortunate not to have fallen into enemy hands. His jet dropped five-hundred-pound bombs and canisters of napalm on the enemy, then strafed them for good measure. Undoubtedly they would have killed him on the spot. I have learned another lesson this morning. I need to learn the difference between the sound of rockets and that of jets.

I return and get my two abandoned water cans. Their contents have spilled, so I go to refill them. As I carry my refilled cans back to my section one more time, I walk by a diesel-fueled generator. Its engine is running and humming loudly. I can't hear anything else.

"BAM! BAM! BAM!"

Rockets strike the ground nearby. A piece of shrapnel strikes the can I am carrying. The can shields my leg from being wounded. The noise from the generator covered the sound of the incoming rockets and robbed me of those precious seconds needed to react and take cover. I learned another lesson: Keep my distance from loud noises. My hearing is a survival tool. For now at least, it is the most important of my senses. My hearing is fine-tuning itself for survival. It already fine-tuned itself to distinguish what type of weapon the enemy are firing at us by the distinct launch noises of their artillery, rockets, and mortars.

The enemy 122mm rocket makes a hollow echoing sound as it is launched. Often the rockets seem to be fired at us in sequence, because their impacts have a leapfrog pattern. Artillery, depending on how far the enemy's gun emplacement is from our outpost, makes a slightly less audible noise when fired. The more prominent the muzzle blast, the closer it will strike to where we are standing when we hear it. Enemy 82mm mortars, the counterpart of our 81mm mortar—the weapon I am assigned to—makes a loud, hollow "TONK" sound when it is fired. Their 82mm mortar rounds, like ours, are dropped by hand down the steel barrel, where they slide to the bottom and strike the fixed firing pin. The mortars have a shorter range than artillery or rockets, so their emplacements are positioned closer to us, to enable them to strike our base. Their mortars are easily heard when fired. When they strike near our foxholes and gun pits, we receive a taste of our own medicine. Their mortars instill the same fear in us as ours instill in them.

Also fired at us is the shorter-range 61mm mortar. When enemy soldiers fire these, they are more likely than not looking at us. It is a close-up, in-your-face type of weapon. Of all the enemy weapons, the 60mm mortar, with its soft, faint noise, is the most difficult to detect, even though it is fired when enemy troops are just a short distance away. We have 60mm mortars in our arsenal.

The loudness of a muzzle blast depends upon the distance to the gun and the angle the barrel is pointing. Not only can I distinguish and identify what type of weapon they are firing at us, now I can determine, by the sound of the weapon's report, what section of our combat base it will strike. It is the rounds that impact too close for comfort that I have trouble detecting. It must be the angle of the barrel. I am learning this by experience. It is sort of on-the-job training.

I am trying not to be careless or foolish. The other Marines in my sector have more guts than I do. They take their time before seeking cover from the smaller 61mm enemy mortar rounds. Some even wait until the last minute to hit the deck or jump into a hole when the larger 82mm has been fired at us and the lethal missile is on its way, shooting through the air, toward our base. Some Marines stand, listening, as the noise of the fins cutting through the air becomes louder, indicating that the missile is coming closer. They dive for cover a split second before impact. It is almost like a game. Who will be the last to take cover? Who is the biggest chicken? I run and jump into a hole when I hear anything. I like living.

Visitors

Mack, my forward observer friend, visits me regularly. I enjoy him because he brings his field maps of Khe Sanh with him. His maps are covered with pencil marks that identify targets he has scouted, then called artillery and mortars on. His radio operator, Holmes, has one goal in mind: to buy a brand new blue 1968 Pontiac GTO. He says he is going to purchase the car through an American car salesman in Da Nang. Car companies like selling cars to military personnel because if a soldier falls behind on monthly payments, it is a simple process to have the soldier's pay garnished by the government.

Whenever Holmes talks about his new car, I wonder how many soldiers in Vietnam purchase cars with hopes of having them in their driveway upon arriving home, only to be killed before ever getting home. I can see a brand new car waiting in a man's driveway, and a mailman walking past it as he delivers the telegram informing the relatives that the proud owner has been killed in Vietnam.

I wouldn't mind having a new Corvette when I get home, but eleven months of my tour remain. Even if I had just days left, I couldn't afford a new car. My monthly base pay for private first class, combined with overseas pay and combat pay, adds up to about $190. That's a little more than 25 cents per hour. I can't even afford the gasoline.

Water

We use water sparingly. The shower, now in pieces, is not a major loss. Even if it hadn't been blown up, who would want to be standing in it naked, all soaped up and waiting for the rinse, during an enemy shelling?

The water from the pumping station is primarily for our canteens. After our drinking needs, sufficient water remains to brush our teeth, shave, and take sponge baths. I store my hygiene water in a plastic mortar shell canister.

After coffee each morning, I take a sponge bath. I take off my combat helmet, which is not a wise thing to do here, and remove its fiberglass liner and camouflage covering. Now I have a washbowl. I have a piece of mirror, compliments of a Marine who smashed his with a rock and distributed the pieces among us.

I don't shave on a regular basis but have yet to be reprimanded by an officer about the stubble on my face. There are more important things on officers' minds here, such as the North Vietnamese Army divisions around us that are intent on overrunning our base.

Dangerous Detail

All our digging has been completed. We have trench lines to provide below-ground passageways throughout our positions. There is little else for us to do but wait for the enemy's next move. With our section of the perimeter completed, I have been assigned to a work detail where I will be doing somebody else's digging. I have been ordered to help dig a new command bunker. The current command bunker's timber supports have been shaken and weakened by concussions from the massive explosions of our outpost's ammo dump. It is feared that the structure will cave in. The new bunker is to be located on the base west of our sector. It will be occupied by officers of my 26th Marine Regiment. I am uncomfortable with the fact that those of us who work on the new bunker will be vulnerable to enemy shelling during its construction.

As we excavate for the new bunker, we shovel the soil into sandbags, which will be used for protection on the bunker's roof. While digging, I let my discontent about being assigned to this work detail be known to everyone around who will listen. The wrong person listened.

The air traffic control tower was the first structure I noticed after I disembarked the airplane. Upon reading the name of the place, Khe Sanh, I immediately got a premonition that something bad was going to happen here.

"Ban Shee," a 105mm artillery piece. The weapon rests upon a concrete slab that gives it stability and provides accuracy when firing. The wooden ammo boxes with the row of sandbags on top are packed with soil and serve as protection from shrapnel from an enemy round.

My foxhole on the eastern perimeter of the combat base, situated behind Bravo Company's trench line. It is marked with my "West Dickens
Avenue" sign seen here in the center of the photo. In the distance can
be seen numerous craters that scar the mountainsides, the aftermath
of bombs dropped by jets and B-52 bombers.

One casualty from the 1200-round shelling is the *Playboy* centerfold we have posted on the door of our ammunition bunker. Miss January has been hit by shrapnel several times. On the cardboard just above her picture are sketches of little "stick men" we used to record our kills.

The 81mm mortar gun pit adjacent to ours. At the moment I took this picture things were quiet—no incoming.

Seigler, already wounded in the hand, talking to a member of the 37th ARVN Rangers. Seigler is wearing the radio headset which is connected by wire to the FDC (fire directional center). By monitoring the radio headset, we are immediately aware of a new target for our mortars. No matter how bad things got Seigler always managed a smile.

Our 81mm mortar. The underlying layer of sandbags are scarred from the first morning of the attack. We added more layers to protect ourselves from shrapnel.

Marines, from left, Urban, West, and Sergeant "Ski" with new stocks of mortar rounds and C-rations. Food and ammunition were priority cargo on incoming supply aircraft.

Flores, left, and Gillim performing maintenance on their mortar. Gillim was later evacuated with wounds caused by an incoming 61mm mortar round. Mark Cool was fatally wounded by a second enemy mortar round while going to Gillim's aid.

The result of a direct hit on one of our ammunition bunkers. This bunker was hit by a 122mm rocket.

Lunch with my spy novel. Here I'm making a grilled cheese sandwich and heating up some instant coffee. Heat tablets, in the oblong cans underneath, provide the fire.

Air support from a jet aircraft strikes close to our lines. On many occasions, the bombs, meant for the enemy, exploded so close that it even caused us to cringe and duck.

Our 81mm mortar rounds exploding on the enemy. The white plumes of smoke are from our white phosphorus rounds; the darker plumes are from high explosive rounds.

An enemy 61mm mortar round meant for me. It was fired at me while I was on the perimeter taking pictures. I was fortunate that I heard the muzzle blast as it was fired. The sound of an enemy 61mm mortar being fired is the hardest to detect. It's very faint. Being that I heard it, it gave me a few seconds to react before the round struck.

The view looking down the base road which roughly paralleled our airstrip. To the right is a "water buffalo" trailer attached to the back of a truck. To the immediate left of the trailer can be seen Khe Sanh's only fire truck. It was used to spray foam on crashed, burning aircraft.

Looking down into the front of my foxhole from ground level. This is where I slept at night. From here I had a panoramic view of the eastern perimeter. Down in the corner is the artillery canister that blew out of our exploding ammunition dump the morning of the 21st of January. It nearly took my head off. I saved it for a conversation piece and an ashtray.

A napalm strike just outside our perimeter. Close-in napalm strikes suck the oxygen out of the air and cause labored breathing when you're too close.

We are under enemy fire. Sometimes the enemy rounds exploded so close (as in this photo) that we had to stand back from our mortar and cringe up against the sandbag walls of our gunpoint to avoid shrapnel and in some instances, bullets.

My address. West Dickens Avenue, Khe Sanh.

An F-4 Phantom jet coming down for a bombing run. We had constant air support both night and day. Sometimes there were so many aircraft in the air space above Khe Sanh that the jets would be in a holding pattern, each one awaiting its turn to come down and drop their bombs.

Looking west down the base road. Clouds enshroud the mountain tops in the distance. In the background can be seen a shot-down CH-53 helicopter and also the wing and engine of a shot-down supply airplane.

Ron amid the rubble of the combat base. He is standing just outside of one of our 81mm mortar gun pits. Off in the distance is the tail assembly of a crashed C-123 cargo plane.

We are under fire from automatic weapons. At this moment the enemy are probing our lines. They are being taken out by the ARVN Rangers down in front of our positions.

Court-martial

I have been summoned by our company lieutenant for complaining about my assignment. I had just descended the last sandbag step into the lieutenant's bunker when I saw him waiting for me. "What's the problem, Corbett?" The lieutenant looks serious and sounds aggravated. I answer: "Why don't these bastards come up from below ground and start digging their own damn bunker?"

My statement doesn't set well with the lieutenant, who threatens me with a court-martial if I don't help dig the command bunker. Rather than face a court-martial, I return to digging, but I continue to complain.

Near the excavation site, I find a wheelbarrow to transport the filled sandbags up a plank ramp. The planks prevent the barrow's wheel from bogging down in the soil that we loosen with our picking and shoveling. After each wheelbarrow of sandbags is pushed up and out of the excavation, we stack the bags in piles to await their use on the roof. Thickness specifications for the new bunker's roof are given to us by the officers overseeing our work. They are hoping to make the roof thick enough to stop an enemy shell from penetrating the bunker. The roof will have double the number of sandbags on the old bunker's roof.

Bunker Work Detail, Second Day

We have dug down five feet below the surrounding grade. I worry that I am working in a large, open target for an enemy shell.

"BAM. BAM. BAM. BAM."

My worst fears about the danger of this work detail are coming true. We are under a rocket attack. I am mad and cursing loudly. I should have faced a court-martial. I dive for cover under the ramp that we use to wheel the sandbags out of the excavation. The ramp is narrow but safer than lying on the open floor of this big hole. Raising my head for a moment, after the first enemy rockets explode, I see the Top, the first sergeant. He is standing behind the old command post we are currently replacing, hanging his laundry out to dry on a clothesline made from communication wire. He is standing upright, intent on completing his chore and seemingly oblivious to the enemy rockets that roar into the base and explode in our area. Is he deaf or crazy? More enemy rockets are coming; I hear them being launched. I claw into the soil that I lie on, wishing I could disappear deep into the earth.

The rockets arrive and explode close by, making terrifying sounds. I am scared as I hear them being launched, then await their arrival. I cringe as each one hits and explodes. They are striking the ground around this hole. It is almost as though the enemy are looking for me. I raise my head to see what is happening with the Top and his laundry.

He is dead, lying flat on the ground under his laundry on the line. I am looking at his laundry as it slowly flaps in the breeze just above his body, as if waving him good-bye. He has been struck by shrapnel, but I see no blood. Perhaps he was struck on the side of his head that I can't see. His body is not moving; evidently he died instantly. At least he didn't suffer. As I stare at his motionless body, I can't believe he died while hanging out laundry. Two Marines come outside the old command bunker to assist him. I already know what they are just finding out.

It has been several minutes since the first rockets hit, and I am leaving this area. I am the only member of the work detail remaining here, because the other Marines hurriedly fled to safer positions. I rise and make my dash. I have lots of ground to cover before I get to our section, and rockets are still striking the outpost. On my way back, I hit the ground twice for cover. I can see our gun pits up ahead and explosions in their immediate vicinity. Dammit. Now my gun pits are under attack. When I arrive I encounter Mills first. I ask him if all are okay. He says that Jeff has been wounded. Jeff and I rode helicopters and a plane into Khe Sanh together; we have been here only one month, but it seems like years. Jeff has lost some fingers. Shrapnel cut them off. He has already been rushed to Charlie Med. As Mills tells me the news, I am smiling. I am happy for Jeff. I remember what the Marine with the bullets in his leg, whom I carried on a stretcher, once told me. I know that Jeff has a million-dollar wound and will be going home alive. The Top will leave Khe Sanh in a body bag.

Bunker Complete

We have completed the new command bunker. Because it is a priority target, we put multiple layers of sandbags on the roof, as we were asked. The finished bunker can probably stand up to anything but a direct hit. There is no safe harbor here. Concrete, the one building material that, if poured to the proper thickness, could stop an enemy shell, is not available. As I look over the fortification, I wonder what its occupants will think of my flimsily constructed foxhole.

ARVN Rangers

I know Vietnamese soldiers by their faces and their straight, short, jet black hair that never seems out of place. They are marching in single file through our mortar emplacements and on past the Bravo Company lines, walking toward the east. A snarling tiger is crudely stenciled on their combat helmets. These are soldiers of the 37th ARVN (Army Republic of Vietnam) Ranger Battalion, a detachment of South Vietnamese soldiers assigned to help us. They have just landed by helicopter and airplane on our outpost. There is no doubt we can use their help, but I see that they are apprehensive as they walk slowly behind their leader. They are being led to the doorstep of the enemy, and they walk as though they are being led to their death. Their presence here is a token gesture.

This small detachment is here with us to fight to the finish. They are supposedly ready to fight with us for their people's right to self-determination; after all, it is their country. Their column disappears slowly into the grass in front of our lines, the same grass where I expect to see the charging enemy. The ARVN soldiers will dig their trench line forward of our positions and construct gun emplacements for heavy-caliber machine guns at intervals along its length.

Although they are supposedly here to help us, I am leery of their presence. I can identify a person of Vietnamese ancestry; their facial features seem so prominent and alike. I cannot, however, determine whether they are from the northern part of their country or the south.

Watching the ARVNs

I have watched them for several days. They make daily water runs through our lines, and I feel sorry for the water carriers, who are slighter of build than I am. Each of their soldiers carries two five-gallon jerry cans filled with water, as I have. As I watch them I think of the stiffness in my fingers from the weight of the cans. I remember my arms feeling as though they were being pulled from my torso. The ARVN soldiers do not complain about their burden, as I have. They steel themselves to their tasks. Some of them stop to rest at our gun pit. Our ability to communicate with them is limited; we know only a few Vietnamese words, and slang at that.

One of the water carriers pulls a bottle of Puerto Rican rum from his pocket. He offers me some and I take a swig so I don't insult him. I return the gesture by giving him an inexpensive ring I wear on my finger. I would like to drink more of his rum, but Khe Sanh is not the place to be intoxicated. Or maybe it really is the place to become intoxicated. I know one thing: It is not the place where I want to wake up with a hangover.

After meeting this man, my mind is more at ease. I learn that there is no reason to worry about the ARVN fighting alongside our enemy. This detachment has already proven itself. The men have fought alongside other Marine units in battles in this region.

Activities

Several activities engage us while we wait for the North Vietnamese to try to take the base from us. One Marine has a cribbage board, and there are several decks of playing cards. Some Marines have radios with working batteries, so we have music. A regulation football can usually be found lying on the ground somewhere around our position. We can look through binoculars and try to locate some enemy soldiers and their positions. There is also weapon cleaning, bayonet sharpening, and letter writing. There is plenty of time to read a new letter or reread an old one. It is better to read old mail than no mail. We can keep up on current events. A Marine on this base who has no idea of what is going on in the world can easily find out. Copies of the military newspaper *Stars & Stripes* are scattered on the ground and in the trench lines. Khe Sanh is front-page news. By reading the articles, we get to relive the events we have already survived. With each new edition, the news about Khe Sanh becomes progressively worse. Thank you, *Stars & Stripes*.

Laundry

Periodically, when circumstances allow, we wash our laundry in boiled water contained in halved fifty-five-gallon steel drums. I have one spare pair of trousers and one extra shirt. The water that is poured into the steel drum washtub in the morning remains the laundry water for the day, and it is used by several people. We boil the water over a fire of discarded wooden ammo boxes; we stir the laundry in the water with a short wooden pole cut from a tent stake. Our clothesline is a length of communication wire suspended above the ground. My military green shirts and trousers don't last long. The jungle utilities I was issued are ripped. I have snagged them on our barbed wire defenses several times. They are also stained from spilled C rations, coffee, grease, diesel fuel, the red Khe Sanh soil, even urine.

The most noticeable odor on everyone's clothes is diesel fuel. When a plane or a helicopter occasionally flies in several bales of new utility shirts and trousers, we are issued a new set. I don't care if the new utilities I am issued are too large. I can hold up my trousers with a piece of rope and roll up the sleeves on my shirt. When I receive new clothes, I immediately burn the old ones in one of our trash fires.

Movies

The movie tent no longer shows movies. It has been abandoned since the first morning of enemy shelling. Ironically, the last feature posted is *Gunsmoke*.

Mark's R and R

My friend Mark from Virginia is going on R and R. He will take his earned vacation in Bangkok, Thailand. The term "R and R" is misleading; it is really not a rest at all. All one does is drink and sleep with the local women every day until it is over. At least it is an opportunity to be out of combat for a week. To rate an R and R, one must have been in Vietnam for seven to eight months.

Mark receives his orders to begin his journey. His first stop will be in Da Nang. Then he will depart on a commercial airliner that will be full of men from other branches of the service who also rate an R and R at this time. I can't think about mine now. It will be a long time coming.

Mark doesn't have civilian clothes to wear, so he will have to find himself a pair of slacks, a dress shirt, and a pair of shoes. I don't have any appropriate clothes to lend him. He will probably end up buying them in Bangkok. Mark shouts to me as he passes my foxhole on his way to the airstrip. "Do you need anything from Bangkok, Jack?"

I am taken aback by his question, wondering how he can think about anything other than getting out of Khe Sanh for a few days. Here he is asking if I need anything from Bangkok. Actually I do. "Yeah, Mark. Do you think you can find an E string for my guitar in Thailand?" He smiles and gives me a parting wave. I watch him leave our area doing the walk we call the Khe Sanh shuffle, a half crouch, always listening for the sound of an enemy gun, always scanning the area ahead for the next foxhole or depression in the ground to jump into. It is a style of walking we all learned here. It is also a nervous condition caused by our environment.

I watch as Mark's helicopter lifts from the steel airstrip matting, then climbs for altitude in circles. It will climb in these circles until the pilot knows he has sufficient altitude to dodge enemy gunfire, then it will fly out and away from this airspace above our base. I watch Mark's chopper become smaller and smaller and finally disappear. I figure he has already forgotten about Khe Sanh.

The Odds

We have about 6,000 men. There are close to 240 Marine officers, 5,500 Marine enlisted, 20 navy officers, 200 navy enlisted (Marine medical corpsmen are naval personnel), 2 army officers, 25 army enlisted, and 1 air force officer. More than half of our numbers are on this outpost. Approximately 1,000—the 1st Battalion, 9th Marine Regiment—hold positions at the Rock Quarry, which is located a mile to the west. Another 1,000—most of the 2d Battalion, 26th Marines— are on top of Hill 558, which overlooks the gap in the Rao Quan River valley, to the north. Two hundred Marines—Echo Company, 2d Battalion, 26th Marines—are covering a ridge between Hill 861 and Hill 558. This ridge, which is considered to be of strategic importance, is named 861 Alpha—861A.

Kilo Company, 3d Battalion, 26th Marines, is on 861 and has already engaged the North Vietnamese on January 19 and 20. The company has just been reinforced with an additional 300 men. Up on Hill 881S are 400 men commanded by Capt. Bill Dabney, India Company, 3d Battalion, 26th Marines, reinforced by a platoon of Mike Company and two 105mm howitzers. On the top of Hill 950, which I see every day because it looms over our outpost, is a single platoon of 50 men from Alpha Company, 1st Battalion, 26th Marines. This is it. We have 6,000 men in seven strategic positions, but miles apart. The 37th ARVN Battalion adds 318 men to our defensive line. We are outnumbered seven to one.

A Reporter

January is nearly over. I am perched on West Dickens, sitting on my sandbag roof and facing east toward the perimeter. In my field of vision are the mortar gun pits and a segment of the Bravo Company trench line, along with stretched-out circular strands of concertina wire, a type of bundled barbed wire that stretches like a giant slinky. It is about 1100. Approximately an hour has passed since the enemy's morning shelling. While writing a letter home, I notice a stationary figure out of the corner of my eye. He has just taken my photograph. He walks over and identifies himself as a United Press International (UPI) correspondent. Lots of newsmen are on the base. Something is always happening for them to write about, and there are plenty of damaged structures from incoming artillery to photograph. Bad things happen here every five minutes.

The photographer asks my name and where I am from. I answer his questions and give him no further thought. In the letter I am writing home, I repeat my old stories. I lie to my relatives about how I am still in Saigon and still get to play golf on weekends. I still don't want my parents to know I am at Khe Sanh.

February

At mail call I receive a large, bulky envelope from home; inside is a folded hometown newspaper. It is a recent edition, and the headline reads: "Vietcong Unleash War's Biggest Assault." Below the headline is a map of Vietnam with Khe Sanh on it. The name Khe Sanh has lots of arrows pointing at it. That's not all that's on the front page. There is a picture of me, with my name and my parent's address. The caption states that I am at Khe Sanh and the picture was taken during a "lull in the action." The news articles on the front page describe our situation. More articles about Khe Sanh are on page two. One article says that we are surrounded by the enemy.

Along with the newspaper is a letter, which I can tell from its penmanship is from my mother. The letter is nasty, so nasty it is almost too hot to touch. The newspaper article stating that we are surrounded has particularly upset her. She has written that she will never believe another word I say as long as she lives. The UPI photographer has blown my cover.

Shouting over to the guys in our gun pit, I ask if any of them cares to see a stateside newspaper. Mills comes over to my foxhole to get the paper, returns to the gun pit, and shares the pages with the Marines there. Not mentioning that my picture is on the front page, I sit and wait for them to see it. I expect a reaction and get one.

"Corbett. You son of a bitch. You haven't been in Vietnam even one whole damn month. How the hell do you rate getting your face in the newspaper?"

Ackerman Is Still Here

Ackerman has not received the paperwork that will transfer him to another unit, the penalty for having waved his Florida state flag at enemy gunners. Ackerman has received a gift in the mail from his friends back home: a battery-powered record player that plays 45 rpm records. There is one problem. Whoever sent the record player enclosed only one record: "Light My Fire," by The Doors. The flip side of the record is "The Crystal Ship." For two days now, since Ackerman received his record player, we have been listening to the same record over and over, mingled with the noise from occasional enemy rocket and artillery shells whistling in over our heads. The lyrics to "Light My Fire" seem appropriate for our situation. The Doors' pulsating guitar music echoes throughout the trench lines and makes things seem surreal. Ackerman must realize that the fire at Khe Sanh has already been lit.

The lyrics on "The Crystal Ship" side of the record particularly bother me. Bracing myself periodically when I hear the firing of enemy guns, I am being serenaded with lyrics about slipping into unconsciousness. All it takes here to slip into unconsciousness is one enemy shell. I can't wait until Ackerman's batteries go dead.

Farewell, Ackerman

Ackerman's transfer orders have been finalized. He has decided to honor me for being his Khe Sanh buddy by asking me to accompany him and help carry his gear to the airstrip. For me to be asked to accompany him is an honor, but it is also a great risk if we come under enemy fire during our walk. We will be going down the open dirt road toward the airstrip, where there is nothing deeper to take cover in than a few tire ruts formed by truck wheels when the road was muddy. There are some foxholes and bunkers off to the side of the road, but it would take extra seconds to reach them before incoming struck. By making this trip with Ackerman and helping him carry his gear, I am cutting his exposure time to possible enemy fire in half. If I decline to accompany him to the loading zone at the airstrip, he will need to make an additional trip to fetch his remaining gear.

As we walk down the road to the airstrip's loading zone, I carry Ackerman's seabag and we both do the Khe Sanh shuffle. We listen for the sound of enemy guns and keep our eyes open, looking for the next place up ahead to hide if we come under incoming fire. We are halfway there when "WHAM," the enemy have fired off a rocket. I find a depression at the side of the road to dive into. Lying here, listening to make certain that no other rockets are being fired and on their way toward our base, I inadvertently stare at Ackerman's seabag. It is several feet away, lying on the road where I dropped it as I dived for cover. I wonder what is in his seabag that I have been carrying for him. Maybe there is his Florida state flag. Maybe his record player. I don't care to know, especially at this moment. I just might lose my temper.

Success

We have made it to the airstrip's loading zone. Our timing is good: A supply helicopter is just about to take off. Ackerman boards, and the chopper climbs in those familiar tight, spiraling circles. Soon it will be out of range of antiaircraft guns and leave Khe Sanh. Ackerman is on his way. Although he caused a lot of turmoil at Khe Sanh, I am saddened that we are going separate ways. Friends are real friends in Vietnam. I have a feeling I will never see or hear from him again.

Nights in My Foxhole

At night when it rains, I am prepared in my foxhole. I have procured several square pieces of polyurethane clear, flexible plastic. Its original use was as protective packing in boxes of mortar rounds. I drape one piece of the plastic against and over the dirt walls of my fighting hole, then extend the excess out and along the top of the original grade to form an apron of sorts. This keeps the dirt walls that I will be leaning against as I sleep from turning into mud as it rains upon West Dickens. To keep dry I place two empty wooden ammunition boxes on my dirt floor, so any water that accumulates at the bottom of my fighting hole is still below the level of my body.

My poncho is too confining. Pulling the hood up over my head interferes with my peripheral vision. If I have ever needed a complete field of vision anytime during my life, it is most assuredly here and now. If I wear the poncho with its hood down, the hood catches the rain. Whenever I pull my head through the neck opening to remove the poncho after a rainstorm, I receive an unwanted soaking. A bath would be welcome, but to wear wet clothes during cold Khe Sanh nights is not conducive to sleep. Still, getting wet does make me more alert and helps me keep an attentive eye out for the enemy at our perimeter.

If I am rained on during the night, I have to wait for the morning sun to appear and dry my clothes. The problem is that the sun does not burn through the fog until late morning. When it finally does, it dries my wet clothes and warms my body. If I get wet during the night and the following day is cloudy, I look for a fire that someone might have lit to burn trash and stand by it until I am dry.

Although the rain is uncomfortable, it does bring me peace of mind. There is something about rain that calms me.

Rodents and Flies

Another nuisance that keeps me awake and away from needed sleep is the Khe Sanh rats. They are big and fat. They find our discarded C rations and eat well. Several times during the nights, while sleeping, I have been used as a stepping-stone by rats on their walks from one food source to another. They wake me when they skip across my sleeping body. They are brazen. They don't attempt to conceal themselves during the daylight hours. Some Marines try to trap them using C-ration peanut butter as bait, and rat traps are a common sight, but the rat population never seems to dwindle.

Several Marines have been bitten by rats. In fact, if someone here makes you mad, one method of payback is to put peanut butter on his toes as he sleeps. Revenge is sweet. Besides rats, we are constantly pestered by swarms of huge green flies. They are always around the outhouses, and they visit our fighting holes at mealtime, so my hands are in continuous motion as I eat. The flies swarm the valley because the bodies of dead enemy soldiers lay strewn outside the base boundaries after hundreds of air and artillery strikes.

Air Strikes

Requesting an air strike on enemy positions is as simple as calling for a taxi, because air support is available day and night. We also have artillery support from several nearby outposts.

Air strikes supporting us are so numerous that sometimes the planes are in a holding pattern; they circle and wait for an opportunity to make bombing and strafing runs on enemy positions around us. The U.S. military strategy is to draw the enemy close to the Khe Sanh base, then unleash airpower on them. This tactical plan is called Operation Niagara. It is a Niagara Falls of sorts, a Niagara Falls of bombs in place of water, falling on our enemy.

Air strikes continue to deface this Eden. The tops of some hills have been completely blown off by high-explosive bombs, which weigh two thousand pounds. A bomb that big can splinter a tree. I haven't seen a bird since the bombing started.

Night Strike

I have been awakened from sleep. A jet descends, screeching loudly in a steep dive. It is dark, so I can't see it. There is no moon. The jet sounds as though it is aiming at me in my hole. As the noise grows louder and louder, I hope the pilot knows what he is doing and hasn't made a navigation error.

Is this plane diving down to drop its bombs on me? I cringe in fear and wish my hole were even smaller than it is. Please don't miss. I am not your enemy. Here he comes. His bombs are dropped. They explode just outside our perimeter. What terrifying sounds. This pilot knows what he is doing. I need sleep.

Nearby Ground

Several craters on the base made by enemy shells are large, and some are near my hole. If enemy shells had hit a few feet this way, my hole would be much larger than it is and I would be dead. I would have been just another casualty for the day, and American television's evening news would have added me to the number of Americans killed for that day in Vietnam. My body, or pieces of it, would have left this Eden wrapped in a plastic body bag.

Protection

We have been shelled for several weeks now. The seriously wounded leave; the slightly wounded stay. I see more bandages, worn on lesser wounds, with every new day.

Shrapnel fragments come in all sizes. Even small pieces inflict a wound. It is not just the size; it is their velocity and where they strike. In fact, preventive measures have been taken to preserve our "family jewels." We are issued flak pants, made of heavy green nylon and meant to be worn over our trousers. They are shaped like a diaper and are heavily padded. Wearing my flak pants gives me peace of mind.

Replacements

The men we lose to wounds and death are not quickly replaced. When replacements do arrive, it must seem to them that they have arrived in Hell. Incoming planes and helicopters are frequent targets for enemy gunners, and many replacements are under fire before they even land. They are here only minutes before someone tries to kill them.

A new guy has arrived to replace Jeff, my friend who lost a couple of fingers and is gone. I can tell that the new guy is just in-country from his shiny new utilities. His flak jacket has all of its fiberglass panels still in place and has no stains or holes. His camouflage helmet cover sports bright patches of green and has yet to be faded by sunlight. The black plastic stock of his M16 rifle has no scratches or scuff marks. He reports to our headquarters and is all checked in and standing in our gun pit, surrounded by several Marines who have been here a while. We are asking the new guy all those small-talk questions that every new guy gets a chance to answer. "Where are you from in the States?" "Do you have a sister?" "Do you have a picture of her?" "Think she needs a pen pal?" "Bring any goodies?"

"Welcome to Khe Sanh," I say to the new guy. Then "BAM." A rifle shot. An enemy sniper has fired and the replacement slumps to the dirt floor of the gun pit. The bullet has ripped through the fiberglass panels of his flak jacket. The panels overlap but are not bonded together. Bullets can, and in his case did, penetrate through the spaces between the panels. A lucky bullet can find its way into your back or your chest. The sniper's bullet entered the new guy's lung. He makes gurgling sounds as he gasps for air.

We turn him on his side so he won't drown in his own blood. We loudly shout, "Corpsman up, corpsman up," a Marine's shout for battlefield medical assistance. As I look at him lying on the dirt floor, I see his body wracked with pain. His movements indicate that the bullet hasn't hit his spinal cord and paralyzed him. That is the good in his bad situation. We remove his flak jacket and cut away his shirt for better access to his wound. His clothes don't look brand new anymore; they are stained with blood. We offer him words of encouragement. "Hang in there, the corpsman is on his way." "We'll get you over to Charlie Med real soon." We repeat this over and over. Encouragement given, our words change. Living here has given us a macabre sense of humor. "You lucky son of a bitch. You're going home already and you haven't even been here five minutes." "We haven't even memorized your name yet." "Can I have your C rats?" "Can I have your jungle knife? You won't need it back home in the States." "So you wanted to be a Marine, huh? See what you get for joining the Marine Corps?"

Standing in a circle, we all have something to say to the kid as he lies wounded and immobile; he is our captive audience. With his eyes fixed on us and in shock from his wounds and our statements, struggling to catch his breath, he hears the most sarcastic member of my squad speak. "Hey, kid, want a cigarette?" Then he is carried off to Charlie Med on a stretcher. We will never see him again. An hour hasn't passed since his arrival; he must have set a record for the briefest stay. I wonder what his memories of Khe Sanh will be. I wonder what his memories of us will be. I should have taken his canteen.

Our Gun Pit

Our gun pit has an ammo bunker attached to it. The bunker is accessible through a door made from the wood of our ammo boxes. There isn't room enough to stand upright in the bunker, so we enter on our hands and knees. On the door of the bunker is fastened the centerfold from the January 1968 issue of *Playboy*. The picture of this beautiful lady, Miss January, has been displayed here since my arrival at Khe Sanh during the first week of January. We don't have the February *Playboy* yet, so Miss January will stay. We have sketched figures beneath her photograph of little stick men in row after row. The stick men represent the enemy soldiers that our mortar has killed; they are called confirmed kills. The stick men become more numerous day by day. We always have some enemy to shoot at because we are surrounded.

7: Under Enemy Fire

Duel

We are under enemy mortar fire. The 82mm mortar rounds are striking the ground by our mortar pits. A North Vietnamese forward observer has pinpointed our gun pits and chosen us as the target.

Our forward observer has located the mortar that is firing at us, and he immediately radios the enemy mortar position to our fire directional center. We have already fired back several rounds. We will attempt to adjust our fire and bring our high-explosive rounds down on the enemy mortar and its crew. There is no doubt that the reason our gun pits have been singled out for destruction by the North Vietnamese can be found by looking at the number of stick men, our confirmed kills, sketched on our ammo bunker door below Miss January. We have killed many enemy soldiers and are a nuisance to the NVA. The North Vietnamese want to kill my squad and destroy our weapon. They have had enough of us. We are good at what we do.

Enemy mortar squads follow the same fire procedures as we do once a target has been selected. At this moment the North Vietnamese mortar men are undoubtedly making adjustments on their mortar's sight, using their near misses as reference points. They will adjust their mortar from these impacts, up or down, right or left. Then they will fire for effect. This is a strange coincidence of war: Their forward observer and our forward observer spot and target each other's gun emplacements at the same time. This has resulted in a mortar duel. It is them or us.

They have fired off another round at our emplacement. The round hits and explodes to the north and to our backs as we face the perimeter. Our forward observer is out there. He has radioed that our first rounds have landed way beyond and to the left of the enemy mortar emplacement. The enemy are currently adjusting the settings on their gun, utilizing verbal instructions transmitted by radio from their own forward observer, who undoubtedly is looking at our faces through his binoculars. I can hear their mortar when they fire.

They fire again. Mortar rounds whistle in and explode on our south side. The point of impact has meaning; all the enemy gunners must do now is calculate and split the difference in distance between the rounds that have landed to the north of us and the one that just exploded to the south. This is called bracketing. When they make this adjustment, they will have our mortar pinpointed. I hear their next round coming. It is whistling loudly as its stabilizer fins cut the air above. The round impacts and explodes at a spot exactly between the two previous points of impact, but it misses our gun pit. Although the enemy have the "to the right" and "to the left" adjustments complete, they need to adjust the elevation. I cringe as I think that the next shot they fire could be a direct hit on our gun pit.

With each exploding enemy round, we duck below the pit's sandbag walls. We are ducking from the shrapnel, and I break into a cold sweat from fear. The enemy are on the verge of blowing up our gun pit, and us with it. I wonder what our forward observer is doing. We can't kill the enemy unless our FO radios adjustments, and we are just about out of time. When the enemy make their final adjustment, we have had it.

Suddenly our forward observer radios the FDC with adjustments, and the FDC gives us new degrees, called "dope," to put on our gun sight. We must adjust our mortar's barrel to fire fifty yards to the right of our last impacts.

Our gunner quickly applies the necessary adjustment, so now it is a matter of which mortar crew fires first—he enemy mortar crew or our mortar crew. It is them or us; kill or be killed. Our next shots are for all the marbles. We quickly hand-drop several mortar rounds down the mortar's barrel, one right after the other. I hope we have fired before the enemy gunners have.

I quickly prepare more mortar rounds, removing all their safeties and adjusting the number of black-powder increments on their tail fin assemblies. I remove all but four of the black-powder increments. Our mortar round doesn't have far to travel to the target; the enemy gun is just over the rise. I wait impatiently for the explosion of our just-fired mortar rounds. "BAMMM." There is a loud, resounding explosion in the distance.

"Nice shot, nice shot!" Our observer reports that we fired our mortar round directly into the enemy emplacement, and the enemy mortar and its crew have been blown up. We somehow exploded at least a portion of their ammunition. We won the duel.

We sketch several more stick men on the ammo bunker door below our *Playboy* centerfold. We are not certain how many men were in the enemy mortar crew, so we have sketched only two. Too bad for them; they fired first.

More Music

The base is taking hits from more enemy rockets. Many are impacting close by us, and I have taken shelter in the trench line, lying on my belly, scared once again and sick of this existence. I hear music. It is Mack. He has taken over as the head of the entertainment department.

Cringing here at the bottom of the trench and flinching as each rocket strikes, I am serenaded by Simon and Garfunkel songs that Mack is playing on his cassette recorder. I listen to the music and the lyrics as I lie here, wishing I were not here. They sing something about being a "citizen for boysenberry jam, Sam," then about an old lady named Mrs. Robinson. If I live through this, someday I might think it was funny.

Instead of writing his girlfriend Patty back in Oklahoma, Mack mails her tape-recorded messages. After she listens to them, she records the latest record albums on the tape and sends them back to Mack. She also records personal messages. I often hear her recorded voice telling Mack how much she loves and misses him.

Lucky Shot

Sometimes, after an enemy shelling, I think about how fortunate I am to have located West Dickens on the lucky spot where the wood chip landed when I tossed it over my shoulder. So far, West Dickens has not been hit. My hole has been missed by their 82mm and 61mm mortars, 122mm rockets, and 130mm and 152mm artillery pieces.

I don't take lightly the fact that I dug my foxhole in this lucky spot. In fact I am becoming as attached as a Marine could be to a hole in the ground.

Ranges

Enemy artillery pieces are out of our mortar's range; our high-explosive rounds cannot reach them. Our 81mm's maximum range is between 2,200 and 3,600 meters, depending on the type of projectile we fire. We have white phosphorus, illumination, and high-explosive rounds. The enemy 122mm rockets have a range of 17,000 meters. Their 152mm artillery pieces also can fire at us from 17,000 meters: 10 miles away. These 152mm rounds leave craters so deep that I can stand inside one and not see over the edge. Their 130mm cannon can fire at us from nearly 19 miles away, whereas our own outpost artillery, a 155mm cannon, can fire only 9 miles. We are outranged. The enemy have the ability, and use it, to fire at us from another country. They fire at us from Laos, which is only 17 miles away. They can blow up our guns, but we cannot reach them.

There are countless pieces of shrapnel lying on the ground at our outpost. No area is spared. On the ground around and in our gun pit are hundreds of discarded silver-colored metal safety pins that we yank from our mortar projectiles to arm them before we drop the bombs down our mortar's barrel. The numerous silver pins are evidence of the many mortar rounds we have fired at the enemy around us.

The Enemy Dig Too

The enemy troops are digging trench lines like ours, but not as deep. They are digging them lengthwise toward our outpost to protect their troops who will charge through them toward us when the time comes. Their trenches are getting closer and closer to our perimeter. During several of the close-in air strikes by our jet planes, and after the planes dropped their bombs, I see an enemy body or an arm or a leg blown into the sky. The body or body part appears momentarily above the mushroom cloud of blown-up debris and smoke, then falls back to the ground and disappears from my sight.

Sensors

We have something our fathers didn't have in World War II, the Big One. At Khe Sanh we have assistance from electronic ground sensors. There are two types of sensors, seismic and acoustic. The seismic sensor detects movement; the acoustic sensor detects sound. Sensors have been inserted along the nearby Ho Chi Minh Trail, the enemy's main infiltration route for soldiers and supplies. Sensors inserted in the jungle surrounding our base transmit signals, which are gathered and interpreted to warn us of an impending attack. The seismic sensors, sensitive to ground vibrations, inform our command when enemy troops are on the move and give our intelligence people an estimate of how many enemy are moving and in what direction. When triggered, the acoustic and seismic sensors provide us with targets. Hundreds of these sensors are placed in the surrounding jungle to the north and west of our base. It is as if we have hundreds of watchdogs around our positions.

February 5, About 0300

We are under heavy fire from enemy rockets, artillery, and mortars, so we worry that the shelling might be followed by a ground attack. It is foggy and dark, and I can't see out too far from my position. Enemy soldiers are attacking the nearby hilltop outpost at 861A. They are charging the Marine positions through gaps in the defensive wire that they have blown out with bangalore torpedoes—lengths of pipe packed with explosives. The enemy soldiers are already inside several of the trench lines. At least seven Marines have been killed. There is hand-to-hand fighting. The army is assisting the Marines by firing their huge 175mm artillery guns from Camp Carroll. The guns we have emplaced on Hills 881S and 558 and the other Hill 861 outpost are all firing in Easy Company's defense. Easy Company, the one under attack, is instructing by radio all supporting guns where to place their fire.

Lang Vei, February 7, 0045

More trouble. The Special Forces outpost at Lang Vei, seven miles west of us along Route 9, is under attack. Lang Vei is the most northerly of sixty Special Forces camps in Vietnam. These camps are positioned along Vietnam's border with Laos and Cambodia. The army's Special Forces soldiers are the professional and intensely trained Green Berets. A Green Beret epitomizes all that you would not want to have as an enemy; they are lethal and courageous. Their only downfall is that they operate in small numbers. There are only a few dozen at Lang Vei. This is not the time or the region to be manning an outpost with a skeleton crew. There are too many enemy soldiers here by the DMZ.

My knowledge of the Lang Vei outpost is limited. I do know that within the Lang Vei compound, Green Beret advisors are in charge of a mixed group of defenders totaling nearly five hundred men. The defenders include companies of Vietnamese and one company of Bru Montagnards, the local tribesmen. Encamped a half mile from Lang Vei are five hundred allied Laotian soldiers. They are disorganized, but at least they are armed.

Lang Vei is transmitting on their radio to the command bunker at our outpost that they have enemy tanks in their wire. Tanks. Their outpost is 1,300 feet long and 400 feet wide in the middle. It is shaped like a dog bone. The NVA have caught them by surprise. Enemy tank crews managed to drive their armor up to Lang Vei's perimeter undetected. At this moment, enemy tanks are driving over and through the outpost's barbed and razor wire defensives.

Word has come that the enemy are again attacking Hill 861A. Our outpost is under heavy incoming fire. Now I hear automatic weapons fire. The ARVN Rangers, our first line of defense down in front, are being attacked. This might be the attack we have been waiting for. Maybe all those red felt-tipped pen lines I saw on the wall map at my orientation are coming.

Word is that the seismic ground sensors are detecting only two enemy battalions. They are approaching our eastern perimeter. The attacking enemy must penetrate the ARVN line first. The next line of defense is the Bravo Company line. Our mortar pits are behind Bravo's trench line. I am waiting in West Dickens. I have plenty of ammo. I have piles of hand grenades with the pins already straightened out for easy pulling.

Could these two battalions be their shock troops, with more enemy soldiers following behind them? We can make quick work of two battalions. All of us Marines are angry. Each of us has pent-up feelings of frustration from being bombarded for the last several weeks and not being able to fight back, frustration at being the target of their long-range artillery and not being able to see them face-to-face.

The enemy can't make it through the ARVN Ranger lines. The Rangers kill the few enemy soldiers that charge their position. The enemy are not mounting a major assault at our sector. They seem to be just probing our lines. Now the movement of the two enemy battalions toward our perimeter has suddenly ceased. I am still waiting to see an enemy face.

The NVA attack on 861A comes to an abrupt halt. Things quiet down quickly—too quickly. Why? It is strange, but fine with me. The attack on 861A and the probe at our end of the combat base perimeter turn out to be just diversions. By their attacks on 861A and our outpost's perimeter, the enemy have diverted our command's attention away from the Lang Vei outpost. It is Lang Vei the enemy want tonight, not us. Can Lang Vei hold out against the tanks?

Now more incoming strikes our base—at least five hundred mortar rounds and a hundred rockets already this night. The incoming is keeping our heads down. The enemy are attempting to keep us from manning our mortar and artillery. They don't want our guns to fire in support of the Lang Vei outpost. We are standing in our gun pit and firing anyway. That is our job. Our mortar rounds can't reach Lang Vei, but we can fire on possible enemy avenues of approach to the outpost. The noise is deafening.

Our outpost is still in radio contact with Lang Vei. Word is belatedly passed down to us from command about that outpost's situation. There are no secrets here. We are all in this together. Things don't sound good for our neighbors at Lang Vei. Each radio transmission tells us that the situation is worsening. What could happen next?

Mortar

We repeatedly fire our mortar. We fire on preregistered targets, and we fire at places we think the enemy might assemble for their attacks. In fact, we fire at anything and everything out there.

Word is that Lang Vei's defenders are firing their light antitank weapons (LAWS) at the enemy tanks and that the shots do nothing more than produce a "shower of orange sparks" as they bounce off the Soviet-built tanks.

Radio reports now say that the Green Berets are trying to knock out the tanks with their 106mm recoilless rifles. Lang Vei's commander is requesting that our base commander send Marines down

Route 9 immediately and come to their aid. His request is denied. Our commander feels that every man is needed here; he expects us to be overrun tonight. Lang Vei will have to stand alone. It is believed that any Marines sent down Route 9 to Lang Vei as a relief force would likely be ambushed and slaughtered. The NVA undoubtedly are waiting in ambush positions along the road.

The tactical but grim decision has been made. Now radio reports indicate that the enemy have exploded Lang Vei's ammunition dump. They are using flamethrowers. New radio reports tell that an enemy tank is on the roof of Lang Vei's command bunker.

The contingent of Bru tribesmen defending a section of the Lang Vei perimeter is caught in a cross fire and is being annihilated. Radio reports state that two enemy tanks are firing point-blank at the doors of the Lang Vei command bunker.

Lang Vei requests that our outpost artillery be fired directly at their outpost. Our outpost artillery fires a top-secret projectile called a firecracker round for the first time. When the round reaches Lang Vei, it impacts on the ground as if it were a dud. It then spews hundreds of golf-ball-sized minibombs over the target area. The bombs then explode as if they are individual hand grenades.

This is a night of firsts. It is the first time the enemy have used tanks on the battlefield, and it is the first use in warfare of the classified firecracker round. Last reports have it that most of Lang Vei's defenders are dead.

It is about 0300 and Lang Vei has radioed another request for help. Then their radio transmissions cease. The Lang Vei encampment has been overrun.

Washington, D.C.

Lyndon Johnson, our president in Washington, has been updated on our situation at Khe Sanh. Word is that the president of the United States is not getting any sleep either; he even has a sand model of Khe Sanh in the White House basement. He gets up in the middle of the night to look at the model of our combat base.

Supply Aircraft

Aside from helicopters, there are several types of airplanes that regularly land on our approximately 3,700-foot-long tarmac. The aircraft bring food and ammunition in their cargo bays. The largest of the aircraft that supply us is the C-130. It has a landing weight of nearly sixty tons. Another airplane that lands at our outpost frequently is the C-123. These are smaller than the C-130s. Occasionally I see a quieter, lighter, and more graceful airplane land and take off. It is called a Caribou. Some planes are silver and some are painted camouflage. The C-130s are called Hercules and the C-123s are called Providers. The Hercules requires the entire length of our outpost's runway to land and take off. The C-123 Provider needs only half the length of the airstrip. Both airplanes have a hydraulically powered rear ramp that is lowered to load or unload.

Many of our supply aircraft are subjected to enemy fire on their landing and takeoff from the airstrip. They are also subjected to enemy shelling while on the ground. So the aircraft maintain momentum, rarely coming to a complete stop. They taxi as quickly as possible to the loading zone near our makeshift control tower. Our loading zone, nothing more elaborate than a wider section of steel airstrip matting, becomes a stage of frenzied activity. Pallets of supplies are jettisoned out the rear of the aircraft, so that the wounded might be loaded. What dead we have in their body bags might be loaded. A Marine whose tour is over might board the plane to go home, or a Marine whose turn it is for R and R might climb aboard.

Because the supply aircraft attract enemy rocket, mortar, and artillery fire, someone at Khe Sanh nicknamed the planes "mortar magnets," and the nickname stuck. Some of the mortar magnets are beginning to run out of luck. I make sure I have a foxhole or a trench in sight and close by when I see a plane coming in.

February 10

I run toward the airplane, which hasn't fully stopped. I don't know how I am going to help when I reach the burning plane. Flames lick at different points on its fuselage. Its engines have shut down, but it is smoking wildly, and the flames are spreading rapidly. Its port-side landing gear collapses, leaving the plane at a downward angle that allows me to see the escape efforts of one member of the cockpit crew. Smoke is thickening in the cockpit.

Mills is already at the plane. He scrambles under the belly of the big silver bird, a C-130 Hercules, frantically searching for a rescue hatch to open and pull out any passengers who might be in the plane's cargo bay. He scurries back out, crawling on hands and knees, from underneath the plane. It is too late. It is too hot. The flames are spreading rapidly. The heat is too much for him to bear. At least he tried to help—more than I. I have done nothing yet. I just stand here, mesmerized by the life-and-death struggle going on in the cockpit. My eyes are fixed on the cockpit crew.

Someone in the cockpit keeps fumbling with the port-side window. He must be groping for an escape latch to jettison the cockpit window glass. His patience must be growing thin. The smoke is thick. The time is now or never for him to make his escape. He frantically kicks out the window, and it tumbles to the tarmac. He sticks his head out; with his back to me, he grasps the window frame and pulls himself onto its sill. He perches there for a brief moment, then releases his grasp and falls headfirst. His back slides down the side of the airplane fuselage. He is upside down as the back of his neck and head hit the tarmac. I think he has broken his neck. It is a long fall from the cockpit window, and he hit the airstrip hard. The remaining members of the flight crew follow through the window. They slide down feet first. They are shouting that there are men in the back of the plane.

Khe Sanh's red fire truck arrives. The crash crew is professional and they swiftly fight the flames with foam, but the fire continues to consume the plane. The flames eat the silver metal before our eyes.

We hear muffled screams from the cargo section. Six servicemen are burning to death. The plane is carrying a flexible bladder of fuel.

There is nothing we can do to help. There is nothing I can do. The chief of the crash crew is standing at the crash site. The plane is still smoldering. There is nothing he can do to help them either. It is February 10, 1968, just another day at Khe Sanh.

Camp Carroll and the Rockpile

It is dark and I can't sleep. I watch bursting artillery flares. They are being fired over our positions by the guns of Camp Carroll and the Rockpile. Camp Carroll is a fire support base located eighteen miles to the east-northeast, adjacent to Route 9. The Rockpile is an artillery base nine miles from us on Route 9. The aerial flares, called star shells, explode just out from and over our perimeter. The flares release a brilliant light. As with the enemy guns, I can hear artillery shells being fired and on their way. When the star shells arrive just over and outside our lines, they ignite, making a loud popping sound. Once ignited, the flares drift down, suspended from tiny parachutes, slowly swaying as they descend. The flares spotlight the area below them. They prevent my imagination from going wild. I know that Camp Carroll and the Rockpile are firing frequently. Their shells enshroud us in a protective ring of exploding shrapnel as they fire night and day. Their gunners must get less sleep than we do. Camp Carroll and the Rockpile are our friends indeed. We are their friends in need.

In my foxhole I take advantage of the light given off by every star shell that is fired from their outposts to explode over our perimeter. I use the light to scan the wire for enemy soldiers. I can't sleep. Awake and watching, I think about the Marine on the stretcher with the million-dollar wound. I think about, and still hear in my mind, the screams of six Marines burning to death in the Hercules.

My mind wanders. My mind and body are exhausted. We have been a target for incoming fire for more than three weeks. I want and need to sleep, but I can't. Instead I find myself just waiting for the sun to come up in the morning. I know it will be hours yet before it rises. As least when it does, this night, like weeks of previous nights, will finally end. The morning will undoubtedly be shrouded in fog as it rolls out of the Rao Quan River valley. It will be late morning before the sun burns the fog away. I wonder what tomorrow will bring.

Bullet Holes

A cargo plane on the tarmac is being patched up. Some North Vietnamese antiaircraft gunners were good shots. This plane has more than 250 bullet holes in its fuselage. These are not friendly skies.

The fate of the Hercules and the loss of other aircraft cause our military to attempt another method of delivery to supply our base. The previous method of landing the supply planes, racing to the loading zone, the frantic unloading and loading of the aircraft, then the plane's race to achieve takeoff speed and fly out, all under enemy fire, is too risky for the aircraft and the personnel.

The new method of delivering supplies is the low-altitude parachute-extraction system (LAPES), which allows planes to be unloaded here but not loaded, because the plane never lands. The plane approaches the runway as if it were going to land, but it maintains an altitude of several feet as it flies down the length of the tarmac. The plane maintains its airspeed while a parachute is jettisoned from the open hydraulic cargo door. The parachute is attached to a sled on which rests the cargo to be delivered. The chute opens, the cargo is yanked out, and the plane, still in flight, continues on its way. The jettisoned cargo eventually skids to a stop at the end of the runway. It sounds logical enough.

One attempt at this method brings another casualty. A cargo of lumber yanked from the airplane continues to skid down the runway at high speed, but the parachute malfunctions. The cargo crashes into a tent at the end of the runway and crushes a Marine to death.

The parachute extraction system has not been successful. Now, supplies are delivered by parachute drops. So far, most of the parachuted supplies have landed within our lines and been retrieved.

War Has No Business Hours

The sporadic shelling by the North Vietnamese is taking its toll on us, both physically and mentally. Whatever energy I have is expended during my runs to a foxhole or a trench line in search of protective cover. This energy, which under normal conditions could be replenished by a good night's rest, is lost. We don't sleep well here. Enemy guns fire sporadically into our perimeter throughout the night. War has no business hours. I haven't slept soundly for weeks. When I do fall asleep, it is from exhaustion. If an enemy shell strikes my foxhole as I sleep, I will not know it. Perhaps I will just wake up somewhere else. Hopefully it will not be in a warm place.

Though I fall asleep when my body demands it, it is never for more than a half hour, because I am usually awakened by an exploding enemy shell. A rocket or an artillery shell slamming into an area of our outpost distant from me produces a muffled sound, as if hearing the trunk of a car being slammed while sitting inside the car with the windows closed. The muffled sound is always followed by an eerie silence. After the incoming strikes, I can't help but wonder whether a round slammed into somebody's bunker or killed someone who was sitting in a hole just like I am. I wonder if this will ever end. I wonder when or if I will get out of here.

My thoughts wander to my family. I wonder what my sisters and brothers are doing. It is two o'clock in the morning here. Home, it is two o'clock in the afternoon. My sisters and brothers are just getting out of school. Or maybe they don't have school today. Maybe it is Saturday. Maybe it's Sunday. I wonder whether I will ever see home again. I want to sit up and scan our perimeter for any infiltrating enemy in the areas illuminated by the star shells. I hope the enemy don't come tonight. I hate that car trunk sound.

Small Pleasures

Finally it is first light. I have recently discovered one of Khe Sanh's small pleasures. I remove my jungle boots and military green socks and let my feet breathe for a few minutes. On occasion I soak them one at a time in water that I have poured into my steel combat helmet-turned-sink. It is refreshing. This simple act seems to make things better, at least mentally. It never fails that while performing my foot ritual I eventually come to my senses. I remind myself of where I am and hurriedly put my boots back on, fearing being caught in renewed action with bare feet. This morning, while sitting with one foot soaking in my combat helmet, my coffee in one hand and a cigarette in the other, an envelope suddenly bounced off my chest. Looking up from my foxhole to find out who threw it, I see Mark. He is back from R and R. "Hey, Mark, you made it. Welcome back. How was Bangkok? Why the hell did you come back here, anyway? You should have stayed down in the rear until things cooled off up here. You're some kind of dumb Marine for coming back to all this shit. Are you crazy?"

Finally Mark has an opportunity to speak. "Your E string is in the envelope, Jack," he says softly. He talks in a normal voice, as if asking me to pass the salt at the dinner table, then he walks away. I am amazed that he remembered my request, made jokingly, for a new guitar string. It is even harder to believe that he took the time in Bangkok to find one. He even remembered that I needed a steel string instead of nylon.

Mark's thoughtfulness to me will not endear him to the other members of the mortar squads. All the Marines within earshot of my foxhole will now have to listen to my guitar playing as I advance, step-by-step, page-by-page, note-by-note, through my Mel Bay self-instruction book. Thanks, Mark.

Saint Peter

Saint Peter is here—Gary St. Peter. He is from Maine. His first name is Gary. I have learned that many Canadians have last names that begin with Saint. Saint Peter is a member of another mortar squad. He was sleeping in the same underground hooch as me on the morning the North Vietnamese first shelled our outpost. He is a low-ranking enlisted Marine like me, so he is also on standby for work details.

Whenever I hear his name shouted—"Saint Peter!"—I pause briefly and verify that I still have earthly surroundings.

A Camera

As I strum my guitar strings inside my foxhole, a Marine passes. Where have I seen his face before? I remember. He looks like the actor on one of the few television shows my father watches at home in the States. He looks like Art Carney, who played Norton on *The Honeymooners*.

I want to let him know who he looks like. Responding to my summons, he comes over to my foxhole and stands on my sandbag parapet, looking down at me. "What's up, Marine?" he says.

"Do you know who you look like?" I ask.

His face begins to grimace. My question has annoyed him. I think twice now about breaking the news to him that he looks like Art Carney. I have a feeling he has been asked this question one too many times. "Yes! I do know who I look like." He sounds irritated. I am sorry I asked him. He is silent for a long moment, then begins to talk once again. "My name is Bob Carney. The actor is a distant relative of mine, so my family tells me."

I feel awkward. Now I notice that Bob has a camera hanging on a strap around his neck. He says he is out and about taking pictures. It is a fine-looking camera. He tells me it is a Petri 35mm with a built-in light meter and a reflex lens that focuses on the picture you want to take. I remember the Kodak mailers I purchased at the PX before the intense combat. Ever the optimist, I had purchased the film when I didn't even own a camera, firmly believing I would find one somewhere, someday, on this outpost. Here is my chance. My camera is hanging around Bob's neck. I am not bashful.

"Can I borrow your camera for a few days when you're done shooting your film? I have a couple of Kodak mailers I purchased from the PX. I'll return the camera. I promise."

Bob says yes. He has only a few frames left to shoot and will bring the camera by my foxhole sometime tomorrow. Though we don't know each other, he doesn't have to worry about me stealing his camera. Where could I hide? He knows I will be somewhere on the base, inside our perimeter of barbed wire defenses. No one here can go anywhere. We are surrounded. Bob gives me instructions on how to operate the camera. The number-one "don't" is "don't forget to take the lens cover off before you snap the picture."

Shutterbug

A man of his word, Bob returns to my foxhole and lends me his camera for two days. My first pictures are of my fighting hole, West Dickens. I photograph it from several angles. I laugh as I snap the photos; I am taking pictures of a hole in the ground. My main objective is to take some action photos. I have two days to get some combat shots. No problem here at Khe Sanh.

My Photos

I almost manage to photograph my own death. While taking pictures on the north side of the Khe Sanh airstrip, I stand at the edge of our perimeter at a point where the terrain quickly slopes down and off into thick elephant grass that extends to the river valley. Past the river valley the panoramic view of ground vegetation abruptly changes as it meets the foothills of the two large mountains that loom over our combat base: Hill 950 and Hill 1015 (the latter is Dong Tri, or Tiger Tooth Mountain).

Through the camera's lens I frame a panoramic shot of the sloping terrain. While focusing the lens and adjusting the aperture to the proper lighting, I hear the faint, soft sound of an enemy 61mm mortar being fired. I am lucky to hear it. There is no doubt that the mortar round is aimed at me; no one else is in sight. I have carelessly exposed myself on the perimeter in the hope of taking a good photograph, presenting my body as a target to any enemy concealed in the foliage.

I hear the stabilizer fins of the small mortar round hiss as they cut the air. With just seconds to react and find cover, I spot a knee-high wall of sandbags, which had been stacked and laid in a straight line. But on which side of the sandbag wall will the mortar round strike the ground? I have to dive against the opposite side to put the sandbags between me and the flying shrapnel. Cringing by the wall and hesitating, I try to determine from the faint sounds of the mortar round where it might explode on the ground. I am almost out of time to dive for cover when I realize that the noise is loudest in my right ear as I face the perimeter. I dive to the west side of the wall, lie flat, and wedge my body against the base of the sandbags.

"BOOM!" The round strikes and explodes on the other side of the wall. It hits the spot where I had been standing. I wait and let the shrapnel fly, then quickly jump up and snap a photo of the smoke and the dirt cloud, the only visible remnants of the explosion. I look for but can't see who fired at me from down in the elephant grass. I lay there, my M16 rifle at the ready, waiting to see whether the enemy soldier will expose himself. He doesn't. He lives to fight another day. I almost didn't.

More

I take other pictures when I probably should not. I photograph my mortar squad during an enemy shelling. It shows them cringing for cover against the sandbag walls of our gun pit. I snap pictures of us participating in leisure activities, and I photograph several ARVN Rangers. Through the camera's lens I manage to take pictures of Marines throwing passes to one another with a football. As they throw the ball, they are undoubtedly daydreaming they are back in the hometowns of their yesterdays.

I am low on film because I have photographed just about everything in sight. I even photographed my C-ration meals as they cooked. I have taken pictures of all the surrounding scenery: the hills, valleys, and distant grassy terrain pockmarked with bomb craters. As I look into the distance through the camera's lens, I see individual blades of grass lose their individuality and become part of a lush green carpet. I have photographed scenes of the base itself, and some scenes of destruction. I have taken pictures of bunkers, foxholes, sandbagged fortifications, and even trench lines, not knowing the names of the Marines who use or dwell within them. I have photographed empty shell casings, rusting metal ammo boxes, discarded combat helmets, boots, gas masks with broken lenses, empty C-ration cans, components of field medical kits, discarded paper of all kinds. If some of my pictures, once developed, are shown to someone who doesn't live here, that person will think they are seeing pictures of a city dump. I have photographed our outpost airstrip. I have taken no pictures of anyone who is wounded. We all have enough mental photographs of that.

On and On

Time is dragging by. The days, never uneventful, no longer seem like twenty-four-hour increments of time. I just exist. On our small plateau, on our dreary, red-soiled parcel of land in the province of Quang Tri, whether it is day or night doesn't seem to matter anymore. In the mornings now, after the regular ten o'clock enemy shelling, we leap out of our trench lines and foxholes, jump up and down, and give the middle finger to the enemy gunners. We shout expletives of every kind; everything that each one of us has in his personal repertoire of insults and obscenities. Our finger gestures to enemy soldiers always make them mad. There is no language barrier when you give someone the "bird." The enemy always respond by firing several more shells at us.

Messages

We write messages to the enemy on the stabilizer fins of some of our mortar rounds before we fire them. The best place to write a message is on the tail fins, because they are the only part of the mortar round left intact after it explodes. We know that the enemy will get the message. Most of the messages we write are simple and to the point, such as "Fuck you."

We write things that would never appear on a Hallmark greeting card. Occasionally, we get personal and write something nasty about the enemy's mother. Writing these messages is something to do, and it gives us a laugh. Soldiers in World War II wrote on bombs. Bombs dropped in the European theater usually had a written derogatory remark about Hitler. Bombs dropped in the Pacific theater usually had a derogatory remark about the Japanese emperor. Vietnam is our war, and we do as we please. We have our own vocabulary, and much of our language is self-explanatory. When a soldier is killed in action, we say he has been "zapped," "fired up," or "blown away." If a soldier is wounded, he "got hit." "Beaucoup" means lots of something, or very large in size. If someone says to me, "Cut me a huss," he is telling me to give him a break. "Cut me some slack" means the same. If you want to borrow money from another soldier, you ask, "How you fixed for jing?" I guess this derives from the fact that coins jingle together in one's pocket. If you want to break off from a conversation, you can excuse yourself with the expression, "I'm gonna beat feet." If you have a plane or a helicopter to catch, or even if you just want to go somewhere else, you could make a cordial exit by saying, "I have to make my bird." The particular airplane that will hopefully, eventually take each of us home to the United States is referred to as the "big bird" or the "magic carpet ride."

Viet Cong is phonetically called "Victor Charlie." Sometimes our enemy is referred to as "Luke the Gook."

The one-to-ten perfection scale we know back in the States is reversed here in Nam. An exceptionally beautiful woman in the States is given a rating of ten; here she would be rated as a one. A ten rating in Vietnam is the worst; a one rating is the best. Anyone who is considered crazy, the Vietnamese call *"dien cai dau"* (pronounced "dinky dow"—crazy in the head). "Listen up" means just that. "Listen up hard" means someone has something important to say and you had better listen. The shouted words "heads up" mean hit the ground and take cover from hostile fire. "Heads up" is one command you don't take literally; if you do, you have an excellent chance of having your head blown off. If a Marine says, "You're boot to me," he is telling you that he has been in the Marine Corps longer than you have.

"Barbecue" means a napalm (jellied gasoline) strike. If someone crosses you, saying the word "payback" to him will make him beware of future revenge. If you intend to really get even, you tell him, "Payback is a motherfucker."

This is our Marine Corps of 1968. My drill instructor told us that in the Marine Corps, "Every day is a holiday and every meal's a feast."

Mind over Matter

The enemy have been shelling us sporadically day and night for more than six weeks. West Dickens continues to be my lucky spot.

The wonderful part of going to sleep here is that my unconscious mind doesn't remember where it was when it fell asleep. In my sleeping moments I could be sleeping in the Waldorf Astoria.

On nights when I am assigned watch at our gun pit, I wear the radio headset and monitor communications from our command center, listening for the command "Guns up. Fire mission. On the guns."

During these watches, it is also the job of whoever is assigned watch to harass the enemy by periodically firing off high-explosive mortar rounds. I like this part. I get to choose the target. I love waking up the enemy. Before I fire the mortar, I look over Mack's forward observer's topography maps. I don't have a plotting board, as our fire directional center does, so I just estimate. I select an area of flat terrain, near a stream or next to the river, where I think the enemy might be mustering or even sleeping, and I point our mortar in that direction. Sometimes I target and shoot at a trail or a possible approach route toward our base. I write my message on the fins of the mortar round and drop it down the barrel. Some nights I remove most of the black-powder increments from the tail assembly of the round so it will strike close by. I listen for the noise of the explosion on its impact. Sometimes I leave all the black-powder increments on the high-explosive round and fire it off, sending it deep into the surrounding jungle, hoping to kill some North Vietnamese. When I am on gun watch, I'm in charge. I like to fire off to the northeast. I don't fire too close to our Marine positions. I don't want to make anyone here more jumpy than he already is. When I leave all the black-powder increments—the propellant—on the round, the blast from our mortar barrel is loud. I have even been told that it is too loud; my harassment fire is harassing the wrong troops. My gun blasts are keeping nearby Marines from sleeping. They want me to remove more increments from the rounds before I fire so the noise won't be so loud. Sleep is a precious commodity here.

After I shoot I always listen for the sound of a secondary explosion, which tells me I have exploded some of the enemy explosives. As yet I have not heard one.

Obstacles

Carefully sown on the ground along our strands of barbed and razor wire are numerous Claymore mines. They are aimed by properly positioning them on their metal legs. The mines have a curved bow shape. They can be exploded from a distance by means of a trailing wire leading back to a soldier who has a hand-activated device that sends a current through the wire. By using this wire, the mine can be exploded at the opportune time to inflict casualties on the enemy. Employed properly, these mines are extremely lethal. The user must be certain that his mine faces the correct direction, or the planned ambush could literally backfire. There is even a printed warning on the housing of the mine itself that reads, "This side toward enemy."

Sewn among the mines are hundreds of trip flares. They are triggered when someone trips over the wires that are attached to the flares. Their light is brilliant. On the blackest of nights they illuminate our perimeter when triggered. The flare's ignition is accompanied with a loud "POP." Though the flares burn brightly, an enemy soldier who sets one off can instantly dash to either side of the lighted area and leave you staring at the flare, searching for him, with ruined night vision that lasts a lot longer than the light from the flare. The flares burn for several minutes. Many times the flares are set off by shrapnel exploding from incoming shells. A fired trip flare immediately draws our attention. We always think the worst—that the enemy have tripped the flare and are on our perimeter. A triggered trip flare makes my adrenaline flow. It is like having a doorbell for the enemy on our perimeter.

Through this maze of barbed and razor wire, trip flares, and mines is a narrow footpath of safe passage. It extends through the entirety of our defensive obstacles and allows us foot access to our forward-most line, which is manned by the 37th ARVN Ranger Battalion.

When I pass for any reason through the minefield using the pathway, I always follow behind another Marine, keeping a safe distance. My mom raised no fool.

8: In Enemy Sights

Knife Throwing

Two types of knives are issued to soldiers in Vietnam, the Ka-Bar (or K-Bar) jungle knife and the standard bayonet that attaches to the barrel of a rifle. The Ka-Bar knife receives its name from the manufacturer, Ka-Bar, of Olean, New York. It was first manufactured between 1941 and 1945 for Marines who fought in World War II. The blade is high-carbon steel and the handle is grooved and made of highly compressed cowhide leather washers. Every one of us has been issued a bayonet, but not everybody is issued a Ka-Bar knife. There are not enough to go around. If you don't have one, you must wait until someone is going home from Vietnam and gives his to you.

I decided to master the skill of knife throwing. I practice hurling my bayonet at a target—a propped-up wooden ammunition box. I didn't know the first thing about knife throwing, including the fact that a throwing knife is balanced and manufactured solely for that purpose. I try to hone my throwing skills. I hurl the knife from a distance of fifteen feet from the target (a wooden lid) and manage to make the knife stick in the lid on a regular basis by using this technique: I grasp the blade between my fingers, so that when I hurl the knife, the point of the blade will be aimed back at me. I keep my arm fully extended while I bring it from behind my body in a curving motion over my head. Then I release the knife. My form is like that of a baseball pitcher using his whole body in a windup.

After moving my target ten more feet away, I discover that I am not a talented knife thrower. I miss throw after throw. I have done nothing other than prove to myself that my bayonet should remain in its sheath or stay fixed at the end of my M16 barrel.

Our Football

Someone carried a football to Khe Sanh. I no longer question anything I see here. After all, I found a street sign. We play football and throw passes to one another. We never choose teams. There are too many holes in the ground to have a real game. Sometimes we throw passes during an enemy shelling. When the enemy fire at us and we have fled to the holes and trenches for cover, invariably someone takes the football along with him. This is when the real game begins. While under enemy fire we hear someone's name shouted. "Hey, Bob. Catch."

Whoever is called is always dumb enough to jump up from cover and try to catch the pass that is being hurled from another Marine in his foxhole. If the intended receiver misses and the ball happens to bounce onto open ground, we all jeer and taunt him until he leaves the safety of his foxhole and fetches it, thereby keeping the ball in play. Our football keeps us amused, gives us some laughs, and keeps our morale up, even if for just a little bit.

Sniper

Only a few days have passed since the North Vietnamese attempted to kill me with a 61mm mortar while I was taking photographs. As I sit on the edge of West Dickens, feet dangling into my foxhole, I practice some basic musical chords on my guitar. The notes sound out of harmony. I must have placed a finger on the wrong fret. Leaning my head forward and down to the left, I look to see which finger is out of place. "BANG." A sniper's bullet has passed through my hair. I felt it. I am stunned and frozen with fear. I was no more than a hair's length away from death. Marines nearby run over to me and form a circle around my foxhole. They all stare at me. "Jack, are you all right? Your hair is smoking."

I am too scared to answer. I place my hand on top of my head and gently rub my scalp. With my eyes closed, I bring my hand back down in front of my face. I slowly open my eyes to check my hand for blood. There is none. Finally I answer their question. "No blood. I guess I'm all right."

It is a good thing that my fingers missed that musical chord. The sniper was probably looking through his scope, had me in the crosshairs while trying for the classic "between-the-eyes" shot, and pulled the trigger in the same fraction of a second that I moved my head to look down at my finger placement on the guitar. My hair is short—Marine Corp style. Close calls don't get any closer than this.

Another Sniper

There are four of us here. I have a feeling we shouldn't have gathered so close together on open ground. At Khe Sanh this goes against common sense. One well-placed enemy artillery round or rocket could make casualties of us all. Our group is exposed to an additional danger; we are on the extreme north perimeter of our base, where we can be spotted by nearby enemy soldiers who are undoubtedly lying in the jungle growth outside our wire. In addition we are standing near where I was recently fired on by the enemy 61mm mortar. We are breaking all the rules for self-preservation and staying out of harm's way. I am uneasy. My sixth sense is telling me something, forewarning me once again. Suddenly, "BAM," the crisp, cracking noise of a sniper's rifle.

A Marine who was just turning his back to us, away from the wind to light his cigarette, screams, "I've been shot. I've been shot." Then he runs around in small circles, like a rat circling inside a cage and looking for an exit. We grab him; we need to find his wound before we can be of any help. He continues to yell, "I've been shot."

His screaming and circling show me he can't be hurt too badly. People don't run around in circles screaming after they have been shot; they usually fall to the ground. Two Marines grab his arms to restrain him. A third Marine pulls his flak jacket off his back. We need to see the wound. First I see a patch of blood, then the intact bullet, most of it protruding from his back. The bullet must have traveled a long distance. Its velocity was sufficient only to penetrate the panels of his flak jacket and prick his skin. The exposed metal surface of the bullet gleams in the sunlight.

The Marine, restrained now, still screams that he has been shot. The Marine who removed the flak jacket puts his fingers around the end of the bullet and quickly plucks it out. Then he turns the wounded Marine around to face him and holds up the bullet, making sure the man sees it. "Here," he says. "Is this what you're screaming about?" In shock and disbelief, the Marine stops screaming. The corpsman arrives and leads him to Charlie Med, and we lie on the ground laughing.

In His Crosshairs

Enemy snipers have been thinning our ranks. Men are being shot while filling sandbags, eating C rations, and relieving themselves. It doesn't matter what you are doing. It matters where you are doing it. It is best not to remain in the same spot too long. We don't want to give a sniper time to spot us and put a bead on us. It is always possible to end up as a site picture in a sniper's scope.

My Turn Again

Enemy incoming is again striking our outpost, and I am in a trench line with Mills and Mark. We have been discussing life, but the shelling ends our conversation. We hear multiple blasts. The NVA are firing rockets, mortars, and artillery. This shelling is heavy. They are firing more rounds than usual. This could be a softening-up phase, trying to make us suffer casualties and keep our heads down as a prelude to a ground assault at our lines. Enemy guns seem to be targeting the eastern sector of the base. Mills, Mark, and I decide that the enemy might launch a ground attack when the incoming stops. If enemy troops assault our lines, I will need my rifle, which I don't have with me. It is a hundred feet away in my fighting hole. Now weaponless, with the distinct possibility of an enemy ground assault, I feel like a jerk. I wait for a lull in the shelling so I can dash to my foxhole and retrieve my weapon. I need just a brief pause from their artillery fire and I can safely cover open ground to West Dickens. As I wait, I hear small-arms fire. The South Vietnamese Rangers, the first line of our defense, are firing at enemy troops assaulting their trench line. Stray bullets, fired at the Rangers by the enemy, pass over our heads. They make buzzing noises when they whiz by, sounding like angry bees.

I look at the Bravo Company trench line in front of our position and see men bracing themselves. They are leaning on the sandbags that lie on top of the trench and serve as a parapet. They rest their guns on the sandbags and aim toward the perimeter. Several Bravo Company Marines look back at me. I can read their minds. They are telling me without talking to come down and join them; the enemy are attacking.

It is time for me to make a move. I climb out of the trench line and run toward my foxhole. My adrenaline is flowing. I run so fast that I hear loose fiberglass panels inside my flak jacket slapping against one another. I arrive at my foxhole, leap in, and grab my M16 and a bandoleer of fully loaded magazines. Anxious about our situation, I am breathing hard. I must return to join my friends in the trench line.

I pause for a moment, listening for the sounds of enemy guns to determine whether it is safe to make my return run. The enemy fire lets up for a moment, so I begin my dash. At first I run across open ground, but then I slow to a fast walk. Although I am listening intently, I don't hear enemy fire. It has momentarily ceased. I walk even slower. That turns out to be a serious error in judgment. My hearing, sensitive as it is, doesn't pick up what I am listening for. The enemy have opened fire again, and I don't hear it. I am only halfway back to my friends in the trench line. I should have kept running. Mack sticks his head out from a foxhole and yells to me. "Come on, Jack. Run. That round's on you. Run, hurry up, run."

Mills and Mark yell, too. Everyone yells for me to run. They have heard a gun firing noise that I didn't hear: An enemy shell that is on the way will strike close by. I am completely exposed on top of the ground. Should I go for the trench line or return to West Dickens? I am back to full running speed and trying to reach the trench line before the round hits. I have about thirty feet to go before I can dive into their trench. I can see Mills and Mark shuffling to make room for me. I will have to do a running dive. I can hear the round whistling in, about to strike.

I am airborne. Between the force of the explosion and my forward running momentum, I am propelled through the air. That is the last thing I remember.

Voices

I hear voices as I regain consciousness. "Turn him over; turn him over and look for wounds on his other side. He's gotta be hit; he's gotta be hit bad."

I recognize the voice. It belongs to Mills. I am coming around. I am more aware now of my surroundings. I am lying on my back at the bottom of the trench. I was blown upward, then down into this trench. My glasses were blown off my face. I don't know where they are. I am five feet deep in the earth on the dirt floor of the trench.

Mills is still yelling to the other Marines in the trench line. "Turn him over and look for blood." I can feel hands trying to turn my body over and find my wounds. The hands struggle but have difficulty turning me over, because the force of the blast has wedged my flak-jacket-clad upper torso between the narrow dirt walls of the trench. I have arrived in their midst in a cloud of dirt, dust, and debris, accompanied by the noise of a terrific explosion. My ears are ringing from the thunderous blast of the rocket. I am in shock. Mills still tells the others to turn me over. I can't speak yet, so I just lie here preparing myself for the onrush of pain that will accompany any wounds I have suffered. Trying to take an inventory of my body, I roll my eyes slowly toward my right arm. It is still there. I can even see my right hand. It still has all five fingers. Rolling my eyes to the left, I search for my left arm. It is also complete with a hand and fingers. So far, so good.

Still flat on my back on the floor of the trench, I try to look down over my chest. I can see the black toes of my combat boots pointed skyward. I still have legs. Now for the big question. I manage to move my right hand. Then I manage to move my entire right arm. I close my eyes and put my hand inside the waistband of my trousers and send it on a mission, ever so slowly, down along my stomach until it reaches my crotch. Yes. Yes. They are still there. Thank you, God. Thank you. Thank you. Thank you. I have passed the field test.

Mills sees that I am coming around. Now he is yelling at me. "Don't move, Jack. Just don't move."

They have finally managed to turn me over to check my other side for wounds. There are none. As I try to stand up, the Marines who witnessed the rocket strike are staring at me in disbelief. They don't believe I am still alive. They are telling me that, if nothing else, I should be seriously wounded. They probably believe that I can walk on water, too.

My head is clear and I have regained my senses. Now I want to see where that rocket hit. I want to see the crater and find out how close it really was to me when it exploded. I climb out of the trench and retrace my steps.

I find the crater at the precise spot where I began my running dive into the trench. I hate to envision what this rocket's shrapnel should have done to me. Somehow it exploded in every direction from the crater—the rocket's impact point—and sliced through the air all around me without striking me. It is unbelievable that not even one shard struck me.

I see Mack nearby. He has found my glasses on the ground by the crater and is holding them in his hand, just staring into space. At the moment, he thinks my glasses are the only thing that is left of me. He thinks I have been blown to pieces; everyone here believes that the rocket should have killed me. I guess I am supposed to be dead, but it wasn't my time yet. It should have been the round that killed me. I can live with the ringing in my ears.

The Ground Attack?

As for the North Vietnamese who attacked the perimeter manned by the ARVN Rangers, they never made it through our lines. The Rangers killed thirty enemy troops as quickly as they could put them in their gun sights.

My earlier doubts about the true allegiance of these Rangers are laid to rest. They fight with a vengeance, because they have received the terrible news that their families have been slaughtered by enemy troops in a nearby village called Phu Loc.

Mail Call

My morale is high today. I have received several letters from home. My younger brothers and sisters write about their problems at school. They write about which teachers they like and don't like. Each letter ends with the same question: "When are you coming home?" The way things are going, I am beginning to doubt that I will ever see home again. My mom sends me letters and packages. In her packages she includes items such as toothpaste, and in her letters she reminds me to brush my teeth. I have awarded my father first prize for what he sends me in the mail. But first, the story behind it.

My dad has a doctorate in microbiology and works for Cyanamid Pharmaceutical Corporation at their Pearl River, New York, branch as a research scientist; he also does some work at Manhattan College in Riverdale, New York, in the Bronx. The faculty at Manhattan College provides him lab space. Periodically, my dad receives a government grant to research a more specialized subject in his already specialized field. The grants are used primarily to purchase equipment. He used the money from one government grant to buy a hi-tech camera that takes pictures through the lens of a microscope. The camera could photograph whatever culture happened to be resting on the glass slide beneath the lens. I understand how this camera makes his work easier. Instead of running back and forth between the microscope table and his desk, he now can just sit at his desk and jot down his observations from the photograph taken by the camera through the microscope. His pictures are worth a thousand steps.

He never uses his grant money, which is a few thousand dollars at a time, to compensate himself for his research. I think I would.

In addition to everything else my dad does, occasionally he submits the results of his research to a scientific journal. Sometimes he even gets published. Dad is a big wheel in the cell world. He tells me he became a scientist because he had no choice. He was struck by an automobile while riding his bicycle when he was a child back in the 1920s. He suffered a severe head injury, which left him with partial paralysis that affected his right leg and right arm. His mother always lectured him that when he grew up he would be unable to do physical labor, such as construction, so he would have to make a living using brainpower instead of back power.

I didn't know my father's father, who died when I was four. I heard lots about him, though. He ran a speakeasy during Prohibition. My grandmother is the one who doled out all the words of wisdom to my dad. She even doled out words of wisdom to me. She has always had something to say. "Don't let money burn a hole in your pocket." "Dress neatly." "You want to grow up to be a hobo and hop trains?" I hated the weekly Sunday drive when Dad took us all to see her. She was always telling us kids that she was a socialite when she was young and beautiful. To hear her talk, she did my grandpa a big favor by marrying him. She still thinks she is the belle of Poughkeepsie.

So, thanks to the driver who ran Dad over, he became a scientist. I didn't follow in his footsteps. There are no scientists here at Khe

Sanh, at least that I know of. My dad and I are literally and figuratively worlds apart. The first letter I received from him contained a brief note about the weather, the traffic he was encountering on the way to work, and something new called "helicopter traffic reports." In the same envelope he sent a copy of one of his published articles, printed by Academic Press, Inc., of New York. "JJ Corbett: Factors Influencing Substrate Utilization by Tetrahymena Pyriformis." Another article under the heading "Experimental Cell Research" was "The Centrifugal Separation of a Synchronous Population Fraction from Cultures of Tetrahymena Pyriformis." I have absolutely no idea what my father writes about. I don't understand a single word of the titles and can't even pronounce the words. Leave it to Dad to send me something like this in Khe Sanh. Little does he know how close I have come, several times, to being blown up and spattered into a billion little cells.

An unexpected but welcome parcel I received came from General Foods Corporation, Westchester, New York. The sister of one of my childhood friends sponsored the gift. She works at General Foods. My childhood friend, her brother, had already been to Vietnam and returned home wounded. In the gift box were several hundred packages of Kool-Aid, enough for every man on the base. In fact, there was enough Kool-Aid to flavor the water of every enemy soldier in this valley. The powder, poured into the water in my canteen, makes the water taste better. General Foods enclosed all the Kool-Aid flavors they produce. Our outpost is littered with hundreds of empty Kool-Aid packages.

Enter Ron

A new person just arrived and reported to our mortar section. Finally I have seniority over someone and can give him orders. It is obvious he is new, because he has pale, stateside skin. It is only February and it's cold and snowing in the northern states. He has been in Nam only the couple of days it took him to travel to Khe Sanh. He has all the trappings of a "fuckin' new guy." His flak jacket, utilities, and camouflage covering on his steel helmet are all unmarred. He will be staying behind in Vietnam the day I leave—providing he survives, providing I survive. Elated as I am, there is something strange about this new arrival. His demeanor and mannerisms give the impression that he has just left Aunt Bee's porch in Mayberry. The guy has no idea what he has just stepped into. He doesn't seem to realize he has just arrived on dangerous real estate. Even the airplane he came in on was under enemy fire. "Hi! My name is Ron," he offers.

"Hi, Ron. My name is Jack. Welcome to Khe Sanh. You better dig yourself a hole in the ground right now, Ron."

"Why, Jack?"

I am right. He just came from Mayberry. I am surprised he has managed to make it safely from the airstrip to our mortar emplacements. Within minutes of my telling Ron to dig a hole, he has his reason why. North Vietnamese guns open fire on our base again. Being a new guy, Ron doesn't recognize the sound of the enemy guns being fired. I will be Ron's tutor.

"WHAM, WHAM."

"Jump in a hole, Ron." Ever so slowly, he walks over and jumps in a nearby trench line. It is almost as if he is daydreaming. He seems naive about the possible consequences. He could have a short life expectancy at Khe Sanh.

The shelling stops. I walk over to the trench line where Ron is hiding and look down at him. "Ron, I know you don't know where you are in Vietnam. For all you know, you could be on an outpost just down the street from Saigon. Let me tell you something. You're not. You're in the enemy's backyard. Now listen up. This damn place is surrounded. There are thousands of North Vietnamese soldiers around us and, guess what, every single one of the motherfuckers wants to kill you. So when I tell you to take cover, you better jump to it."

9: They've Come to Kill Us

February 23, 1968

Things can't get much worse. We are being shelled again. The first enemy rounds of this barrage find Ron, nearly a week at Khe Sanh, still taking his time running for cover. If he is going to get killed or wounded, so be it.

The shelling is more severe than usual. It is sustained. It seems as though the enemy have opened fire with every gun they have. The muzzle blasts from their gun barrels merge into a rolling crescendo of thunder. This attack is bad. I am away from my foxhole because I am digging a new length of trench line. I will take shelter here rather than chance returning to my foxhole over open ground.

Ron is next to me filling sandbags, and I am looking at him and wondering how he will react to the sounds of these enemy guns firing. He doesn't react. I yell at him to lie down in the trench for protection. He is nonchalant, acting like an idiot.

Numerous rockets, mortar, and artillery rounds are coming in, and I am worried that this might be the big one, the one before an all-out enemy ground attack. Shells and rockets strike and explode close by our trench, and I am lying in the trench in a cold sweat. There are several near misses that explode at ground level, just to the sides of our trench. It seems, at least to me, that enemy gunners are determined, once and for all, to blast our base into oblivion. I am scared. How long can my luck hold out? I thought I was used to this; after all, I live here. Shrapnel whizzes as it cuts through the air above us. Its hissing and zinging intensify my fear, and I claw the dirt floor at the bottom of the trench, trying to make myself go deeper into the earth than I already am. The earth is the only refuge we can turn to and hope will save us. Raising my head to check on how Ron is doing, I can't believe what I see. Ron is standing and looking around as if he is a spectator at a ball game. What is wrong with this guy?

"Listen up again, Ron. I'm not kidding around. Get with the damn program. This is not a park. If you want half a chance at seeing home again, other than in a body bag, start eating dirt like I am. These people are trying to kill you. Now get with it, you fool."

I stun Ron with my harsh words. He lies down in the trench line. The incoming is getting worse. We lie on our bellies, head to head, our combat helmets almost touching. I am thinking about dying. I am almost certain that I won't survive this one. It is time, I decide, to make some arrangements of sorts. I don't want to die without a final good-bye. "BOOM." Yes, it is time. Raising my head, I see the new camouflage covering on Ron's helmet. He hasn't said a word. He is realizing that this is a place of life and death. I think he is scared now, too. I feel bad that I yelled at him. I need to make some final arrangements, and I will need Ron to do that. "Ron, this is pretty serious incoming. If by chance I don't make it, I want you to get a message to my parents, brothers, and sisters, back in the States. I'm from a town called Nyack. It's in New York state. It's spelled N-Y-A-C-K. When you get back home to the States, if you do, I want you to tell them I died a good Marine. I want you to tell them I died quickly and didn't suffer any pain, no matter if I suffer or not. I'll do the same for you, Ron, if you get killed here today."

Ron does not respond for a full minute. Perhaps he is still mad about my yelling at him. I was only trying to help. Ron slowly extends his hand over the dirt floor of the trench. "Shake on it, Jack."

Survived Again

We made it through the shelling. I saw the sunset. It is night; I am in my foxhole, and I feel shell-shocked. Some Marines say the enemy fired 1,400 rounds at us today. Others say they fired 1,700 artillery rounds, rockets, and mortars. To me, that means the enemy tried to kill everyone here from 1,400 to 1,700 times today. However many rounds the enemy fired doesn't matter. It takes only one to make you dead.

Ten dead Marines are wrapped in plastic body bags and are lying on the side of the airstrip to start their journey home to America. Another sixty are seriously wounded but fortunate to be alive. They wait for helicopters, our ambulances in Vietnam, to evacuate them. The less seriously wounded are tended by corpsmen and the medical personnel at Charlie Med. Some of the wounded return from medical treatment to their positions wearing blood-stained bandages. All of the less seriously wounded are no doubt disappointed that they didn't receive the million-dollar wound—a wound just serious enough to have them evacuated out of here. I don't blame them.

My Shower

It is raining. I have never seen it rain as hard as it does in Vietnam. It is called the monsoon. I feel as though I am standing inside a car wash. Today I consider the heavy rain a gift from Mother Nature, because I need a shower. The warm temperature of the rain makes it pleasant.

Our water usage is rationed. Although we have water to drink, we don't have sufficient water to bathe. It has been weeks since I have had a shower. I am going to make this rain shower my shower, and I will be quick about it. I don't want to be caught naked under enemy fire.

I hurriedly take off my flak jacket, flak pants, utility shirt, trousers, boots, socks, and helmet. I lay my weapon to the side and go out in the rain. I stand naked for all the world to see, friend and foe alike. I feel so dirty I don't care if enemy soldiers see me. I soap up and cover my body with suds. With each scrub I feel brand new. The large rain-drops feel refreshing as they pelt my skin. I am one large soap bub-ble. I haven't felt this clean in weeks. Now I am ready to rinse. It has stopped raining! It is as if someone turned off a faucet. I am stand-ing here covered with suds, arms outstretched, cursing at the sky.

Laughter comes from men in my squad. They think it is funny. I don't. I will be spending the night sleepless, scratching my body, which will be itchy from the dried soap.

Foods

Hamburgers, hot dogs, and pizza don't exist here. I haven't seen a sandwich since the morning of the first attack. We make do with canned rations. The main food staple of the enemy is rice. The Viet-namese eat roots, vegetables, and plants that grow in the jungle. They eat taro leaves and manioc (sometimes called cassava). A cassava bush can grow eight feet high with roots to three inches thick. Sweet potatoes and corn are cultivated by villagers. Banana trees are abun-dant, but the fruit is miniature compared to the bananas I see in mar-kets back home. Chiquita wouldn't put a sticker on any of these. There are thickets of sugarcane where one can hack off a section, crack open the stalk, and suck on the sugar. When I suck on a piece of sugarcane, I feel energetic.

The meat from a water buffalo has excellent flavor, but it is scarce. Water buffalo are used to till the fields, so if you kill a villager's water buffalo, you take away his "farm tractor." Fish are plentiful in the many rivers and streams throughout these mountain highlands. The enemy and we have plenty to eat.

More Bad News

It has been several days since the heavy shelling. Word is that aerial reconnaissance photographs show the NVA trenches coming closer toward our perimeter. That is no surprise, because we have been observing lights outside our base boundaries for the last several nights. We think the lights are from miners' helmets that the enemy soldiers wear to see where to dig in the dark. We worry they might dig tunnels under our defenses to the center of the base and possibly emerge at night in our midst, ready to fight. We are apprehensive about another option the enemy have: Dig a tunnel to a spot inside our lines, stockpile explosives, then explode them.

The enemy's night digging bothers us. Back home, America's news media is hinting that Khe Sanh could be America's Dien Bien Phu. Leading the North Vietnamese is General Giap, the same general who engineered a victory for the Vietnamese over the French in Dien Bien Phu. He surrounded and laid siege to that outpost fourteen years ago.

Here at Khe Sanh, Giap is using the same siege tactics he used at Dien Bien Phu: digging.

Air Strikes

American fighter jets make continual bombing and strafing runs. When the jets drop canisters of napalm on the enemy, close to us, the exploding jellied gasoline makes a loud swishing sound on impact as it ignites. The closer impacts, just outside our lines, spew warm, heated air in our direction. I feel it. Our breathing becomes slightly labored, because burning napalm consumes great amounts of oxygen, stealing some of what we need to breathe. When I see napalm strikes, I think about the enemy underneath the flames.

Fighter jets that fly here to assist us carry a mixture of ordnance: high-explosive, point-detonated impact bombs of all weights, and canisters of napalm and rockets fastened to bomb racks beneath the wings. Most fighter jets have guns for strafing.

Although I wouldn't want to be an NVA soldier, I don't feel any sympathy for them. Like me, they have come here of their own accord. They come, knowing we are here. They come to kill us, and they have come in strength; the electronic ground sensors indicate that.

It is all so strange. We are in a beautiful valley, a garden of Eden. This scenery will come to mind whenever I hear the word "paradise." It is beauty we can't enjoy; we all live underground.

Patrol

It is morning on February 25. The commanders want to send out a patrol from Bravo Company to locate and destroy an enemy mortar emplacement. The mortar crew has been singled out because of the excellent marksmanship of its crew.

The commanders have got to be crazy. It is going to be nothing but a suicide mission. This will be the first patrol to leave our perimeter since the NVA attacked. I look at the men who are going on the patrol and I see Marines all locked and loaded for bear: hundreds of bullets and a stash of hand grenades on each soldier, two machine gun crews in their ranks, 1,800 bullets each.

The Marines from Bravo are in formation on the southwest perimeter. They are calm before the storm. This is not a morning to die.

It will be only a matter of minutes before they make contact, because the enemy are just a short walk away.

I watch them step off the base, ever so slowly, through a gap in the circular strands of razor and barbed wire defenses. I run back to the gun pit and join my squad; I know it will be only minutes until their backpack field radio sends out transmissions pleading for help. We stand in the gun pit, ready. We prepare multiple high-explosive 81mm mortar rounds and lay them in our gun pit. The gun is level and sighted to fire on the first section of terrain that the patrol must cross. If necessary, we can fire along the sides of the path they are now walking. We have pulled the safety pins from the mortar rounds excepting one: the safety pin that self-ejects from the mortar round as it leaves the barrel. The tail assemblies of the stockpiled mortar rounds are nearly bare, because we removed most of the black-powder increments from each round. We don't need all increments for this mission; these rounds won't have to go far. The patrol won't get that far.

We can swing the mortar tube to fire in another direction at another target if need be. Our barrel has a ball-and-socket connector at its bottom, where it meets the circular metal base plate.

Other targets don't matter this morning. Our concern is to assist the Marines on the patrol in search of the 60mm enemy mortar crew that has been highly accurate.

Ambush

Bravo's twenty-nine-man patrol started its mission, and its radioman has transmitted his first report. He radios that the patrol has spotted three enemy soldiers walking down the road of the Khe Sanh village coffee plantation. The patrol will try to take the men prisoner.

As the men in the patrol sprint after the enemy soldiers, they are lured into an ambush, caught in a cross fire of enemy automatic rifles. The patrol is taking casualties. One Marine has been shot in his left eye. The corpsman has been shot in his chest and kneecap. One squad of the patrol is attempting to flank and circle behind the enemy emplacements. The squad is, at this moment, being slaughtered to the last man.

I hear the gunfire in the distance. The sound of the unrelenting automatic weapons fire is joined by the loud blasts of exploding hand grenades thrown by the Bravo Marines and the enemy. Bravo needs help.

A fifty-man relief force goes to the Bravo patrol's aid, but it is prevented from linking up. It has run into a blocking force set up by the North Vietnamese. Now the relief force is under heavy automatic weapons fire. The men are pinned down by mortar, rocket, and machine-gun fire. Pleas for help come from the Bravo patrol's radio.

Some Bravo Company Marines who were not required to go on the patrol are positioned down on the perimeter, just beyond our gun pits. They are following the grim reports of their comrades' situation. They are extremely upset and gathering together. They are also raging mad. They can hear the gunfire as well as we can. They are determined to rescue their Bravo brothers.

Our regiment commander refuses them permission to go. They are furious. I watch as one Bravo Marine, still inside the outpost, draws his bayonet and raises it high, attempting to incite the others to disobey the commander's orders and follow him off the outpost to their brothers' aid. There is anger, frustration, and confusion in their ranks. The regimental commander still refuses to let them go. He doesn't want to send them to their deaths. He is aware that they would probably be slaughtered, too.

We fire our mortars. We are firing faster than we have ever fired before. I hear our mortar rounds exploding in the distance. I hope they are on target and are helping.

Our base artillery opens fire to assist the Bravo patrol. The sounds of automatic rifle fire in the distance start to taper off. That is a bad sign; it means it is almost over for those men. Dead men don't fire weapons.

Jet fighters are striking the enemy positions.

Later

Some men from the relief force got away from the ambush and stumbled back to our outpost. They report that probably no one is left alive at Bravo's ambush site. They say the jets dropped their bombs and napalm too close to Bravo.

A corporal from Bravo's patrol is carrying the patrol leader's body and the patrol's field radio. The corpsman, shot in the chest and kneecap, made it back by crawling here. He crawled for three hours.

Twenty-five Marines are dead or missing in action, and their bodies are only eight hundred yards from us. No one here can bring their bodies home without putting themselves in danger. One man, Ronald Ridgeway, was taken prisoner by the North Vietnamese.

February 25 Evening

I stare blankly at the perimeter even though, after what has happened this morning, I should be looking hard. Staring into the darkness, I wonder if anyone who went out on this morning's patrol could still be alive, lying wounded at the ambush site. There is hardly any talking among the men on the perimeter. Any feelings we had have been numbed.

I recall the faces of the Bravo Company Marines as they stood on the edge of the perimeter this morning, waiting to go. They are all dead now. I knew, and they knew, that they wouldn't live to see this night. The patrol found the dragon.

Undoubtedly I am not the only person thinking about the possibility that someone could be lying out there alive, waiting for us to come for him. The Marine tradition of always retrieving our wounded and dead from the battlefield has been shaken. Our dead are still out there.

Acceptance

I am resigned to my existence, to sleeping in a hole. Being here is giving me insight into what is really important in life: simply being able to live. I have slept, eaten, and sought shelter in my hole from the bombs. I have arranged and stored personal possessions in my foxhole as if it were my house or apartment. I have lived like this for a month. I hope I don't leave here in a body bag.

We are low on water. There is no chance of breaking out of here and walking toward the coast. The enemy outnumber us and would repeatedly ambush us if we tried to leave. Their artillery, rockets, and mortars would follow and bombard us as we walked.

We are not leaving because our orders are to hold our positions. Leaving on foot is out of the question.

Rumors are that the NVA's trenches leading to our base are complete. Their main trenches branch off into tertiary trenches that will disperse assaulting troops along our perimeter. The enemy are here.

B-52s

We have had hundreds of fighter jet and artillery strikes in support of us, but the enemy are still here and not withdrawing. With trench lines complete, their attack must be imminent.

The U.S. Air Force is sending huge B-52 Stratofortress bombers to help us. The planes are above us and dropping bombs close to our lines. They fly so high we can't see them or hear their jet engines, although each bomber has eight engines. We hear a horrific screeching, tearing noise—the sound of bombs falling. They sound as though they are ripping the sky apart as they plunge earthward. Of all the sounds of war I have heard, nothing is as terrible as this.

It is a frightening but beautiful sound, because the bombs will kill many enemy soldiers. Shock waves ripple from the bombs' impact. The valley trembles. In the target area, off to the east, giant clouds of debris blow into the sky as the bombs explode. The bombs rip a swath of devastation below and parallel to the bombers' flight paths; the swath in the earth reveals the direction of flight. Each bomber carries up to thirty tons of bombs of varying sizes. A single two-thousand-pound bomb can leave a crater thirty feet deep.

The sky in the valley hazes as it fills with a fine red dust from the massive, multiple explosions. We get to breathe the dust of death hanging in the air.

Everyone has jumped from the trenches and foxholes clapping, whistling, and cheering for the bombers. It is as if it's a ball game and our team has just scored. I guess it has.

"See Ya, Charlie"

The B-52 strikes continue on a regular basis. The bombers fly missions day and night. Sometimes they drop bombs close to the base. With each strike, I feel my chances increasing for leaving Khe Sanh alive.

When the bombers drop their loads near our hilltop positions, some Marines open their mouths and scream to equalize the effects of the bombs' concussions. I hope our pilots don't miss their target and bomb us. If we can't see them, I know they can't see us except on their radar.

Now that the enemy are the target of B-52 bombers and subject to their relentless, awesome, destructive firepower, they must hurry and attack us or leave. If their divisions remain in the region, they will be annihilated. Even near misses by the B-52 bombs cause casualties. The concussions from the explosions cause enemy soldiers to bleed from their orifices, because their bodies hemorrhage inside. The B-52s are turning the tide of this battle.

Mack

Mack is pursuing a correspondence course in journalism from the University of Oklahoma. His lessons arrive periodically in the mail. Upon receiving them, he diligently studies for several days, interrupted only by an enemy shelling or his duties as forward observer. When he completes a lesson, he mails homework to his teacher at the university, who corrects his work and mails it back to Mack. Mack's homework is often riddled with red ink; even I know what that means. Sometimes I feel bad for him, especially if he has had a rough day being shelled or shot at. Maybe if his teacher knew he was at Khe Sanh, she would lighten up with the red ink. I hope Mack is successful in journalism. He will have lots to write about if he survives.

Mack hasn't been talkative lately. On a recent afternoon when things were unusually quiet, we were having a conversation outside our foxholes and trenches. I was only half listening to what Mack had to say. I was listening more for enemy artillery or mortar fire. I was certain I heard enemy artillery fire and convinced myself that an enemy shell was in the air and on its way. The other Marines, all talking, didn't hear the gun's report. I yelled the warning, "Incoming, incoming!"

Everyone dived for cover except Mack. He just stood there. When I realized that he hadn't heard my warning, I shoved him hard into the trench and jumped on top of him. No artillery round crashed into the outpost. Mack was lying beneath me screaming that I broke his leg.

He hasn't talked to me for several days now. He can hardly walk. I don't know what it was that I heard, but it sure sounded like enemy artillery. Maybe it was a dud.

Necklace

The Marine who was shot in the back just walked by my foxhole. He is no longer screaming that he has been shot. He has a big grin on his face as he displays a chain around his neck from which hangs the bullet that was once in his back. The medical personnel at Charlie Med made him a necklace. What next?

Crashes

An observation plane takes off from the airstrip. As it climbs, its engine sputters, then fails. The plane loses momentum and falls back to earth uncontrolled, crashing on the south side of the perimeter. Its fuselage is crushed on impact. The whooshing sound is followed by a column of black smoke from burning fuel. The pilot has been killed.

A giant CH-53 helicopter hovers above the airstrip's loading zone. The pilot gradually tilts the nose of his aircraft, gaining forward momentum for his takeoff toward the east. An enemy shell explodes on the ground immediately beneath the helicopter. It looks from here that a second shell has struck the starboard side, and I see a hole. The whirling rotor blades of the helicopter disintegrate before my eyes. Shards off the huge blades are hurled out and away in all directions by centrifugal force; the blades were spinning at full takeoff power. The helicopter falls to the runway, burning. Khe Sanh's red fire truck is making its second appearance. Again, there is nothing anyone can do.

Looking toward the southern horizon, I see a spotter plane painted military green. It must be out there scouting. It is flying alongside a high ridgeline, level with the top of the ridge and cruising slowly on a southerly course and away from me.

"CRACK, CRACK, CRACK." Enemy antiaircraft fire echoes in the distance. The spotter plane's port wing rips off the fuselage and the craft plunges to earth as if it were a stone. The pilot must certainly be dead. There is no rescue. I don't even mention it to anyone.

Patty

It is night once more, and our water cans are empty. I am in the gun pit and things are quiet so far. Mack decides to use the silence to dictate a letter on his cassette recorder to his girlfriend Patty, back in the States. I can hear each word. He says sweet things to her. He is so calm, he could be calling her from Miami Beach. He whispers into the recorder's microphone: "Hi, Patty. Everything is fine. I just figured you might want to hear my voice . . ." Several minutes into the recording he becomes more and more intimate. I move away because he is getting too personal. "BOOM." An artillery round explodes nearby. The sound is recorded on the tape. Mack is at a loss for words and stutters, because he has just told Patty how quiet things are.

I have had enough of his verbal letter. I bang on the sides of our empty water can and yell into the can for an echo. "Hey, Mack, ask your girlfriend if we could have a glass of water." Mack is not talking to me yet. He is still angry about my pushing him into the trench.

Cooking

I have mastered methods of preparing my C rats. I can heat a meal quickly by using plastic explosive. A pinch of C4 burns at a higher temperature than the heat tabs that come with our food. The C4 boils water in seconds. It is not dangerous as long as I let the explosive burn itself out. I can't step on it to put it out or it might blow my foot off.

Occasionally we make a meal together. Each of the participants contributes a can of food from his own stock. A contribution with gravy and meat is welcome. Cans of ham and lima beans are not allowed. We combine our donations and cook a "Mulligan stew" in a metal ammunition box.

Just Thinking

There is plenty of time to think at night. I think about many things while I sit in my foxhole, waiting for the enemy to attack. The nights when all is black and no one is around to talk with are lonely. Other Marines are in their own foxholes, trying to catch some sleep between the noise of occasional incoming shells and the friendly bursting star shells. Sometimes I think about walking over to the trench line for a chance to lie down and stretch out. My West Dickens hole isn't long enough for this. In it I need to bend my knees and pull my legs back to lie down. I always decide against seeking stretch-out comfort in the trench because my foxhole has been such a lucky spot so far, protecting me from enemy shells.

Because it is night, I am not daydreaming; I am really dreaming. My mind continually wanders; it is an escapism of sorts. So what if my body can't safely step off the base? My mind can leave.

I don't know what other Marines might be thinking. Their minds undoubtedly wander off the base, too. In solitude, I wonder whether there is really such a being or an entity as God. I know there must be thousands of religions in the world, with different beliefs and different names of gods. Followers of different faiths always look to the sky when they pray. He must be up there somewhere, I guess. People don't stare at the ground when they pray, unless bowed in a respectful position of submission on a prayer rug. Religions give God many names. It seems to me that there is a God for every letter of our alphabet, from A to Z: Allah to Zeus.

When I arrived at Parris Island, I left religion on the bus. I didn't bring God with me to boot camp because I went there to learn to kill.

Reinforcements?

Hope of assistance from other units is slim. During the recent celebration of Tet, the Vietnamese New Year, the enemy launched massive, coordinated attacks on military outposts, major cities, and villages. It is not safe anywhere in Vietnam at the moment. Reinforcements aren't available. We are on our own.

The stress of being here is getting to me. Several men have been evacuated from the base because they suffer from shell shock. I will try to stick it out.

Sights

As I walk around the perimeter of the outpost, there is not much to look at other than bunkers, foxholes, trenches, and weapons. Along the barbed wire, stretched along our southern defenses, one defensive structure stands out. If awards were presented for the most original bunker, this one would win. It is a long, sandbagged structure with numerous portals through which Marines can fire their rifles. The roof of the fortification is covered with sandbags.

Covering the sandbags on the roof are yards of soil, compacted and leveled. Protruding from the portals are the barrels of various weapons; there are some M60 machine guns, and out of the center portal sticks the barrel of a .50-caliber machine gun. I wouldn't want to be an enemy soldier charging this bunker. The Marines who built this were prepared.

Could This Be It?

Our commanders believe that the enemy will attack on the last day of February. All indications are that they have completed preparations for their assault. If they wait for two more weeks to attack, it will be the anniversary of their first attack on Dien Bien Phu. Their trenches are within 350 feet of our lines. Ground sensors are showing more enemy troop movement than usual. Colonel Lownds put the base on full alert, and we have been ordered to gather by the gun pits for a situation report.

There is silence as we muster for the meeting. Sergeant "Ski," who has a long handlebar mustache, and Sergeant Williams give the briefing. The two sergeants, standing side by side, whisper to each other. By the looks on their faces, it seems that something is weighing on their minds. The two men were briefed on the situation earlier. Now, whatever is going on will be passed down to us. Both men are tough Marines who never flinch during incoming, and they always look out for the men. Twice under incoming fire, Ski and I dived for the same foxhole. Sergeant Williams likes to play cribbage in the trench lines.

Situation Report

Sergeant Ski speaks first. "Men. Tonight's the night. Intelligence tells us the enemy completed the final phases of their buildup and is ready to strike. We're outnumbered seven to one. The Pentagon is aware of our situation. Every man is to fill all their M16 magazines and keep hand grenades at the ready. You men from mortars: When they charge through our defenses you're to point your mortar tubes nearly straight up in the air and kill as many charging enemy as possible. Retrieve our dead and lay them in the trenches. If you're wounded, and the enemy is running over and through our lines, fake dead the best you can. On a given signal, after they've charged through our positions and carry their attack to the center of the base, those of us on the perimeter who survive the initial assault are to rise, turn about, and encircle the enemy and annihilate them. I wish you all the best of luck. I'm proud to have served with all of you. With God's help we'll see each other again in the morning when the sun comes up. Semper Fi. Do or die. God Bless the Marine Corps!"

Sergeant Ski's speech is over. We look at one another in silence and disbelief. We pair off. It is time to go to work. I will be with Mack tonight. We will defend my foxhole together, and we will fight to the finish together. We have been good friends. You may as well die next to somebody you get along with.

Our mortar will be manned by a skeleton crew consisting of the squad leader, the gunner, and one ammo man. The squad leader will wear the radio headset to monitor orders from the fire directional center (FDC). The FDC will tell us at which targets to fire. If the situation report is true, our mortar will fire off hundreds of rounds tonight. We stock high-explosive, illumination, and white phosphorus mortar rounds inside the ammo bunker. We can blow up, light up, or burn up.

Mack and I prepare for whatever comes during the night. We quickly establish a plan. It is decided undemocratically by Mack, who has been in Vietnam more than two and a half years and seen much more combat than I, that he will be the main shooter. I am to keep his M16 magazines full as he empties them at the charging enemy. He will toss the empty magazines in my direction for refills. Mack and I have about thirty magazines between us. They are already filled with bullets. For speed, some of the magazines are taped together in pairs at their bottom ends. When one magazine is emptied, all the shooter has to do is grab it, remove it from the weapon, flip his wrist, and insert the other full magazine, taped to the empty one, into the weapon. The shooter can reload in seconds.

Why Wait?

Our mortars, the artillery on our base, and the huge 175mm artillery pieces from Camp Carroll and the Rockpile aren't waiting for the enemy to strike first. All open fire at possible avenues of enemy approach. Gunfire is also concentrated on areas where ground sensors detect enemy movement. There are strong signals from the sensors in the Lang Vei area, where the Special Forces camp was overrun. More sensors come to life and signal that the enemy are approaching Khe Sanh village. The ground sensors are being triggered in sequence, indicating that the enemy are approaching the east side of our base perimeter. The ARVN Rangers will see the enemy first, then Bravo Company, then Mack and I. The enemy will be coming right at West Dickens.

We have placed our hand grenades within easy reach. Our knives are ready. Some Marines even have shotguns. Our preparations finished, we wait.

While each pair of Marines reviews their strategy for the looming battle, something strange happens: Marines on the perimeter begin laughing. The laughter is proceeding slowly up the trench lines toward us as it carries from one Marine to the next. I don't know what they are laughing about. I don't think our present circumstances are funny at all. Who could just laugh off a situation like this?

Finally a Marine yells over to me: "They forgot to tell us what the given signal was." Now that's funny. I laugh, too. I pass the word and hear the laughter continue along the perimeter.

What isn't funny is that the joke will probably never make it all the way around the Khe Sanh perimeter, because there are considerable gaps in our lines where a Marine can't see another Marine, let alone pass a message. That is no laughing matter.

Whatever the "given signal" was intended to be is of no consequence, because the plan doesn't sound good, at least to me. To rise from our positions and try to encircle the NVA in the middle of the base after they breach our defenses and overrun us could prove to be double massacre; in the darkness, friend would be indistinguishable from foe.

Mack and I have made our plans. Because he is a forward observer, he has a map and a compass. We come to the conclusion that we will be the only two survivors. Optimism is an amazing state of mind. Mack's plan is for us to make it down to the Rao Quan River—after the battle, of course—and follow its banks through the jungle until it eventually leads us out of the jungle highlands and to the sea. I play the plan through my mind several times; each time I do, it sounds less feasible. How could we cover the ground from the base to the river with all these NVA in the valley and around our positions? Mack's idea sounds good in one respect, though: We would have water to drink, and I would finally be able to take a bath.

Word is that two flights of B-52 bombers have been diverted from another mission and are flying to our aid. They will drop their bombs eight hundred yards from our perimeter. They use radar and onboard computers to pinpoint their targets, and I hope they don't miss. Their bombs could obliterate the base and kill us all.

In the darkness I can't see other Marines in the foxholes and trench lines, but I know who is there. We face the unknown—and the worst possible ending to the time we have spent here—if the attack comes. I know many Marines defending our lines just by their nicknames. Somewhere on the lines, down in front of me, is Texas Mex, from Texas; Jesse, from Culiacan, Mexico, who enlisted in the Marines so he could become a U.S. citizen; Chief, a Native American; and Pineapple, from Hawaii. Also waiting in the darkness for the enemy to come are Smitty; Steve Riddle; George Swanwick; and our black soul brothers, Mitchell, Jones, Holmes, Wright, Thomas, and Scott. Brons is here from Chicago, Courtney is from Des Moines, Ron from Nebraska. Somewhere out there are Bill and Mills from Pennsylvania, Bob from Florida, Wayne from Georgia, Louie from the Carolinas, Hoppy from St. Louis, Alvin and Jim from the Bronx, Mark from Virginia, Byrnes from Oregon, and Jim from New Jersey. Mack is from Oklahoma and I am from Nyack. Saint Peter is out there somewhere, too.

During these bleak moments, the words "United States" take on a special meaning to me. On Khe Sanh's perimeter, we *are* the United States. We intend to fight and die together. We will die as one. We will kick some ass before we die. The enemy will pay dearly for our lives.

Some Marines are here because they got in trouble as civilians back in the States. A judge gave them the choice of going to jail or joining the Marine Corps. Undoubtedly there are Marines here who wish they had chosen jail. Jails don't have incoming and aren't surrounded by enemy troops.

Fighter jets make flights every few minutes and drop their ordnance just outside our lines. When the enemy come, I will set the selector switch on my M16 rifle to full automatic, and as the enemy come closer I will switch to semiautomatic. In the semiautomatic mode I will take aim on one NVA soldier at a time, then fire and quickly go to my next target. If I am overwhelmed with too many targets, I will throw hand grenades.

I hear automatic weapons fire down at the ARVN trench lines. I am anxious as I wait for thousands of enemy soldiers to emerge from the darkness. The noise from the rifle fire gradually subsides. Our allies, the ARVN Rangers, repel the enemy assault. Only about a hundred enemy have charged the line. Though the fighting is close by, I don't see one enemy face, because the darkness and the sloping ground keep the ARVN line out of view.

Is this just an enemy probe? Are they testing the strength of our lines? Where are those divisions of enemy soldiers?

It has been quiet for two hours since the enemy's initial assault. Only about thirty minutes are left in February 1968. This month should have been over yesterday. It is a leap year, one additional day in the month.

10: Home Is Where You Dig It

More enemy charge the ARVN lines. They are again shot down by the Rangers. The enemy are sacrificing themselves. They must be stupid to send so few soldiers to attack us, a Marine regiment. But maybe there are few left to attack our lines. Maybe the bombers have done their job. The North Vietnamese around us were targets for hundreds and hundreds of jet and B-52 bomber strikes. Camp Carroll and the Rockpile have gotten their share; their guns are never silent. Our base's heavy weapons, even our mortars, have taken a toll.

March 1, 1968

Last night was slow in passing. I am exhausted from lack of sleep. At first light I see the bottoms of Hills 950 and 1015 but not their cloud-enshrouded peaks. The fog from the Rao Quan River valley, where Mack and I had planned to flee, rolls up in dense patches to our plateau. After what the sergeants said last night, I didn't expect to live to see this scenery. The Marines, last night concealed in darkness, once again have faces. I enjoy this new day that I thought I would never see.

March is no different from February. The enemy begin the month with the same routine: the morning shelling, the midday shelling, and the before-we-go-to-bed shelling. We fire. They fire. Some Marines place more sandbags on their foxholes. My foxhole will remain untouched; I don't want to change my luck.

I am leery of enemy snipers. They fire more shots at us than before. I wear my combat helmet and remove it only to give my scalp some needed fresh air.

I wrap my M16 rifle and its magazines in an undershirt to protect them from the fine dust created by the dropping bombs. The M16 is high precision; it takes little dust to foul and jam its movable parts. I don't like to think that my weapon might malfunction at a time when I need it most.

Ironically, the enemy weapon that I fear the least—the 61mm mortar—is inflicting casualties in our section. The enemy mortar men are accurate.

March 2

I am filling sandbags on the south perimeter for a bunker that needs more on its roof.

"BAM, BAM, BAM." Here we go. I dive for cover from enemy shells. I raise my head and see incoming mortar rounds exploding near our gun pits. I hope the men in my mortar section made it to cover. I need to go back to our gun pit, because we will have a fire mission.

I run, crouched over, listening for enemy gunfire, scanning my surroundings, looking for the next hole to jump into while on my way. I am doing the Khe Sanh shuffle. Coming to my mortar section, I don't like what I see. Several Marines are rushing to a spot between two gun pits. That is a bad sign. No one groups up unnecessarily during incoming fire. Something has happened. Three men are lying on the ground by Mark's gun pit. They have been hit by shrapnel. Mark is one of them. He has taken shrapnel in the head. Two Marines, wounded in the legs, moan in pain.

The Marines with the leg wounds were caught in the open by the same 61mm mortar round. Mark went to drag the men to safety when the enemy mortar fired again. This second round exploded next to Mark, blowing him to the ground with a head wound.

Mark is lying there trying to wake himself, as if from a dream. His eyelids flutter as he fights to come to consciousness. Marines yell, "Corpsman up, corpsman up!" Mark is going into a coma. The men carry him to Charlie Med.

Word is that Mark succumbed to his wounds after being evacuated out of Khe Sanh. It is said that he fought his way to consciousness one final time. I don't believe that Mark will get a medal posthumously for his deeds; one that his relatives could have for a keepsake. There were no officers around to witness his heroism. We who knew him decorated him in our hearts.

I am tired of waiting for an enemy who never come and for a battle that never starts. I am numb with the thought that Mark is dead. Surely, if he lived, he would have been a tremendous asset to his hometown, his friends, his family, and even to his home state of Virginia. I make myself a promise that if I survive Vietnam and ever have a son, I will name him Mark.

By the light from the star shells, I can see fog rolling up to our lines from the Rao Quan River valley. I am in a mental fog; I can't sleep, so I stare at the perimeter, searching one more time for the enemy. I am half staring and half dreaming. A light rain begins to fall, just enough to make me damp and cold. Looking at our gun pit, I can see the mortar's barrel pointing skyward, propped up and resting on its metal legs. I can hear more star shells coming out to us. They explode, and flares come down on parachutes, swaying to and fro on their way to the ground. In the flare light I see a poncho over our mortar barrel to protect it from the rain. The poncho bulges where it covers the barrel and its metal legs. The poncho's hood is at the top of the mortar barrel and drapes down. It makes a silhouette like a hunched man. I feel that I am looking at the grim reaper, who forebodes death to come. For the first time at Khe Sanh, I feel the intangible entities of hope and optimism slipping from my spirit.

I hope Mark's spirit is in a better place. If there is such a thing as a final judgment, I know he will pass the test. Thank you for the guitar string.

March 6

The fog is as thick as cotton. I am having coffee in my hole. Another night of sleep taken in morsels brings brief respite from exhaustion. I hear the sound of airplane engines under strain and at full power. Planes can't land in this zero visibility fog. The noisy engines disturb what was until now the tranquil morning. What's up? What now? The engines are getting louder and the plane is coming in my direction, but I still don't see it. The plane has everyone's attention. All eyes are peering into the fog.

Then, engines straining, the plane emerges from the fog at nearly ground level. The pilot needs to gain altitude so he won't crash. He is flying too low. The plane is coming at me. I jump into my foxhole afraid it might hit me. I see the pilot in the cockpit. His face is close to the canopy. He is trying to see the airstrip in the fog. He missed it. It is several hundred yards to the north; he is parallel to it. I can't see it in this fog. For a fraction of a second, I make eye contact with the pilot. In a vain effort to communicate, I jump up and down on the ground, extending my arms out from my body and flapping them up and down like a bird. I am trying to tell him to gain altitude.

Its engines whining at maximum speed, the plane passes over our positions, climbs, and disappears into the fog, heading west. It doesn't circle or make another attempt to land. The noise of the engines fades as the plane flies away. I worry that it will crash into one of the hills—950 or 1015, Tiger Tooth Mountain. The quiet returns to our morning.

Word is that a C-123 cargo plane was hit by enemy antiaircraft fire this morning while flying over Khe Sanh. The crash killed everyone on board: four airmen, forty-three Marines, a navy corpsman, and a civilian photographer named Robert Ellison. Word is that the photographer wanted to return and stick it out with us.

News of the plane crash haunts me, and I wonder whether it was the plane that flew out of the fog at our positions.

Guard Duty

I am a sentry tonight outside of Colonel Lownds's bunker; he is commander of the base. I am grouchy. Sleep is a precious commodity here, and I haven't had much.

Ron will share the night watch with me. I have a choice of first or second watch, because I have seniority. I select first watch. Ron can sleep during my watch and I will sleep during his.

I have a bad attitude. Not only do I dislike digging other people's bunkers, I dislike guarding other people's bunkers.

I spend the watch on my feet, staring out from the middle of the base, seeing nothing but shadows and the dark forms of fortifications. I stand, because if I sit I will fall asleep—I am that tired. Periodically I twist the top off my canteen, position each eyeball in turn snugly against the spout, raise my head back, and let the water soak my eyes. This keeps me awake.

Ron's Watch

Finally, my watch is over. It is 0200 in a black, no-visibility night. It is so dark that I wouldn't be able to see an enemy soldier until he stood next to me. There wouldn't be time to say "Halt! Who goes there?"

Although it is Ron's watch, he is lying on the ground using his helmet for a pillow, right at my feet, and snoring. The sleep fairy probably has him far away from this place. Maybe he is dreaming that he's at lovers' lane with his sweetheart, or dreaming he is reading a menu at a nice restaurant.

It is my turn to sleep and time to bring Ron back from wherever he's dreaming he is. It is time to bring him back to a bad reality and wake him up to Khe Sanh.

There is only one way to awaken a sleeping Marine at Khe Sanh: very gently. I don't want to startle him, because I might get stabbed or wind up on the wrong end of a smoking M16. I tap Ron softly on his flak jacket, but there is no response. I tap him a little bit harder. Nothing. I am tired, I need sleep, and I am losing patience.

"Get the hell up, Ron. It's your watch." I shout so loud, I might have awakened the colonel. Ron lies motionless at my feet. I am irritated. This is his watch. I haul off and kick Ron's head with my jungle boot.

A raving maniac jumps to his feet. We are fighting right in front of the colonel's bunker at 0200. Ron has both his hands around my throat and starts to squeeze. The bastard is so strong that I can't pull one of his hands away with my two. He has such a tight grip on my throat that I couldn't apologize if I wanted to. He has cut off my air. He has the strength of a crazy man. He is not letting go and I think I am turning blue, but I can't tell because it is dark.

Thankfully he releases his grip. He looks at me for a moment and says, "I can't kill you, Jack, after all you've done for me." I am glad I did something for him; otherwise, on this night, I would have been killed at Khe Sanh by a maniac instead of the North Vietnamese.

The Pile

"BAM, BAM, BAM." The shelling continues, and shrapnel whizzes above us. It appears we will be in this hole for a while.

This is wearing us down mentally. A Marine brother is at the bottom of our human pile moaning and talking out loud: "Oh God, why are you doing this to me?" I am lying on top thinking that it is not God doing this to him. It is the North Vietnamese. There is a brief pause, then he sobs, "I'm never gonna make it out of here alive." His statement shakes me. We are all on the edge of despair, but we have hidden it, until now. His spirit is broken. Lying here on top, I want to comfort the man at the bottom. He needs encouragement. "Don't worry, Marine. We'll all leave here alive. We're all going to see home again. When we do finally get out of here, you're going with us." The sobs stop. He has heard me.

I said this only to comfort him. I really don't believe what I said.

There is good news and bad. The bad news is that a Marine took a direct hit by an enemy 61mm mortar round and the projectile embedded itself in his torso. The good news is that it didn't detonate and he is still alive. He is at Charlie Med, where they will operate and try to remove the round without detonating it.

The medical personnel at Charlie Med do some quick thinking about how to perform such a dangerous operation. They place the man on the operating table and stack sandbags around him, hoping that if the round blows up during the operation, the sandbags will help contain the blast. Next, they suspend a mirror from the ceiling above the operating table. Using the mirror for visual guidance means that it is not necessary for them to stick their heads over the sandbags to see what they are doing. The risk the surgeons take is the possibility of having their hands blown off. The operation is a success. They remove the mortar round without detonating it.

Luck

A Marine shows me an M16 magazine with a bullet hole in it. The ammo clip was in his flak jacket pocket over his heart. It deflected a sniper's bullet. Some are lucky and some are not. Some Marines are killed by enemy shells and their bodies blown apart so bad that there is not much left to gather and put in a body bag.

We have been dodging incoming shells for more than six weeks. I am no longer scared of dying, although I fear an ending that is painful or lengthy. What I fear isn't death. What I fear the most, and am terrified of, is not living. I am too young to die. I have a lifetime in front of me, or at least I once did. There are lots of things I would like to do yet. I have dreams that I would like to see come true. If I get out of here alive, I will appreciate things in life that I have taken for granted.

After sleeping in a foxhole, I decide that when I die, I don't want to be buried in a hole. I choose cremation and want my ashes scattered above the ground.

Enemy Ordnance

One weapon the enemy have not used yet is airburst artillery. I don't know if they have this type of ordnance. It is a high-explosive artillery shell with a timer. Instead of exploding on impact, the round can be calibrated with a wrench and timed to explode in the air, above the target. If these were used against us, our casualties would be greater, because the shrapnel explodes downward, and shards could hit us in our roofless trench lines and foxholes. If the enemy had them, I think they would use them.

The American military command in Vietnam keeps a score-board of sorts. There is a daily "body count" of those killed in action during the previous twenty-four hours. The daily tally of friendly casualties is accurate, but enemy casualties are estimated. The body count is sent to the news media, which in turn relays it to the American public. That is why I say it is a scoreboard. What can't be shown on the nightly news are territorial gains. We don't have front lines. Jungle warfare is conducted in obscure battle-fields, which soldiers either walk to, are driven to, or are inserted into by helicopter to become victors or vanquished, wounded or body bagged. Things might be peaceful when we exit a helicopter, but once we have walked away from the insertion point and far-ther into the jungle to "snoop and poop" or "beat the bush," it is only a matter of time before we find the enemy or the enemy find us. Usually the enemy find us first, because they see our heli-copters coming from miles away.

President Johnson is worried about the Vietnam War, which he inherited when he took office. He is especially concerned about what is happening at Khe Sanh, which has been on the nightly news for two months now.

The majority of my generation is against the Vietnam War. There are even Vietnam veterans in the States joining protests against this war they have left behind. Sometimes, it seems as though all of America is against this war. My dad is even against it, but we never agreed on anything anyway.

We would feel a lot better here if the American people were behind us. I would feel better if at least my father was on my side. Yet although this war isn't popular, and few rally in support of us, the growing antiwar movement doesn't bother me that much. I am in Vietnam of my own accord. I enlisted in the Marines for adventure and to find out what I am made of. I have achieved both goals. It is definitely an adventure, and I have found out that I am a chicken.

President Johnson asked the Joint Chiefs of Staff to sign a written guarantee that the North Vietnamese will not overrun our combat base. The president should send the guarantee to the Marines living here. We would sign it; we are not leaving until the war is over.

Though outnumbered seven to one, I am confident I can kill my seven, and even help another Marine kill his seven, before I am killed. Besides, with our 81mm mortar, our squad has killed more than our seven each already.

Mail

My father mailed me an old issue of *National Geographic* magazine. Why would he send me an issue that is two years old? Does he think I have nothing better to do than read *National Geographic*? But as I glance through the pages and see photos of the Vietnam of two years ago, the reason my father sent this particular issue becomes clear. On page 298 of the September 1965 issue is a photograph of the Khe Sanh plateau taken two years before my regiment came here. It is a pretty place.

My mother's letters still remind me to brush my teeth.

As Days Pass

Mack is still limping with his leg injury caused by my pushing him into a foxhole. Most of us have jungle rot: cuts and scrapes that don't heal. The skin won't close over the wounds and they become infected.

Foxhole Status

West Dickens Avenue is still a lucky hole; although it has had near misses, it has not taken a direct hit. It is showing signs of wear from continual use. The soil floor is compacted from my jumping in and out of the hole, and I sleep on it. The dirt side walls are baked hard by the sun; loose soil no longer trickles down them. The piles of soil shoveled out when I excavated the hole have settled and now blend with the surrounding terrain. The sparse vegetation that once grew around my foxhole is dead. Perhaps the weeds and grasses decided to wait for better times before making a comeback.

Whereas my foxhole shows signs of use, the surrounding ground shows signs of abuse. Metal splinters of jagged-edged shrapnel of all shapes and sizes carpet the ground. Thousands of tiny steel flechettes cover the area. Lying among all this is unexploded ordnance, complements of our blown-up ammo dump.

There is not much paper litter. We burn it along with the wooden ammo boxes we don't have use for. We burn discarded clothing and all trash that is flammable. We even burn "Dear John" letters. We light our trash fires on foggy mornings so the enemy can't distinguish the smoke from the fog.

Helicopter and airplane carcasses litter the sides of the airstrip There are crashed aircraft in the mountains and valleys beyond the boundaries of our combat base. At the more obscure crash sites, the remains of the crews lay within the wreckage.

Surprisingly, some of us still have a sense of humor, and humorous signs randomly appear. The signs are printed on a plank or a piece of cardboard. In my area there are several signs that stand out; they read, "The Alamo," "Appearing nightly the Rockettes," "Home is where you dig it." My favorite sign is posted over the entrance to a bunker. It reads, "Room for rent." Many Marines write on the back of their flak jacket and on the camouflage covering of their combat helmet. I saw a Marine wearing a metal button that read, "Does Vietnam exist?"

Mack's Ship-Over Talk

I believe it only because I saw it. Not only did I see it, I heard it. In the Marine Corps, when your active-duty contract is about to expire, the Corps has special personnel who attempt to persuade you to reenlist. The verbal sales pitch is known as a "ship-over talk." The potential reenlistee is enticed with such offers as an immediate thirty-day leave, the promise of a cash bonus paid in one lump sum, assignment to a duty station of choice, and a promotion. For each four years of active duty, the Corps also awards you a stripe, called a hash mark, to attach to the sleeve of your uniform.

I was with Mack when he got his ship-over talk. Listening to the benefits the ship-over officer promised Mack if he would reenlist, I felt as though it was Christmas. It sounded wonderful—until the enemy started shelling us again.

The shelling continued about as long as the ship-over talk. When the officer was done, Mack said, "Let me think about it." If it was my ship-over talk, I would have told him to go to hell.

Smoking

Our "smoking lamp" is always lit. When I light a cigarette at night, I cover up with my poncho, so the match doesn't reveal my whereabouts. When I take a drag, I cup the lit end of the cigarette between the palms of my hands, hoping there is no enemy sniper around to put me in his gun sight. Occasionally, several of us sit inside our ammo bunker to smoke. We close the wooden door and hang a piece of canvas to prevent any ray of light from escaping. We position a shining flashlight on the floor close by for light. We discuss the latest rumors and talk about what we are going to do when our turn comes to go home. We talk about our dreams in life, all the while hoping that we will get to live. We talk about that "some day," the day we might get out of Khe Sanh. Survival is always on our mind. Yet here we are, smoking inside an ammo bunker.

March 23

Good news. The numerous bombing missions by American planes have inflicted tremendous losses on the enemy around Khe Sanh. Word is that the North Vietnamese are beginning to withdraw their divisions.

The enemy still bombard us. Today they fired more than 1,200 mortar, rocket, and artillery rounds at the base. When the incoming slams the base and explodes, we take cover, even though we realize there is no safe place to hide.

Endurance

I am still mentally sound, although the enemy shellings are extremely stressful. Some of my fellow Marines are not faring as well. We have lived like this for more than two months. For some, it is a bad dream; for others, it is a nightmare. There are times I feel as though I have known no existence other than eating out of cans and jumping in and out of holes and trenches.

If I wanted to, I could get myself medically evacuated from the base with a rat bite. All I would have to do is remove my boots before I sleep, spread peanut butter on my toes, and hope that a rat took the bait. I would be evacuated for rabies shots.

Another way to get evacuated is to "accidentally" shoot myself in the foot. I don't feel comfortable with that either. If I am afraid to let a rat bite my toes, why would I want to put a bullet in my foot? Rather than either of these options, I prefer to take my chances with the enemy.

Centerfold

One casualty from the 1,200-round shelling is the *Playboy* centerfold we have posted on the door of our ammo bunker. Even though it is March, Miss January is still up there, and she has been hit by shrap-

nel several times. Two of Miss January's most attractive assets have
been "wounded."

Direct Hit

An artillery round has struck a command bunker, penetrating the
layers of fortifying materials on its roof; the round rocketed through
and exploded inside. It is the bunker I helped build, next to the one
where the Top was blown away hanging his laundry to dry. I almost
got killed on that work detail. Seven Marines inside the command
bunker die. I hate to think what an artillery round can do to my foxhole. All the extra sandbags didn't help the command bunker.

Shaving

I shave about once a week. It doesn't matter to me whether I die with
a beard or a clean-shaven face. Shaving turns my razor red. The red
Khe Sanh soil has penetrated the pores of my skin. My clothing is
red. I am red too.

Looking Around

Looking west-northwest, we see parachutes dangling from shattered
trees, their silk canopies snagged before they completed their descent to the ground. Our supplies are air-dropped. Other parachutes
lay scattered randomly on the ground, their canopies deflated and
flattened to awkward shapes.

The once picturesque Khe Sanh valley looks like the surface of
the moon. It is scarred by craters of all sizes and shapes, depending
on the size of the bombs that dropped, exploded, and gouged it.
The craters are mostly round, but some are long and oval. Some
craters are teardrop shaped. These craters are on the slopes of distant hills. There are fire-blackened patches of soil from the napalm
dropped by fighter jets. The many air strikes have killed human life

and plant life. Someday plant life will return. These human lives never will.

Media

Thanks to television's nightly news, the American people are aware of Khe Sanh. They must be weary of having watched news footage of this base every evening for the last two months. You can photograph the same wreckage from only so many angles before it becomes boring.

The American people have had enough. General Westmoreland plans to send a relief force to get us out. The military operation that will be carried out, in unison, to relieve us at Khe Sanh is named Operation Pegasus. Pegasus is a winged horse in Greek mythology. All military efforts for our relief at Khe Sanh are considered part of this operation. Ground troops are coming north toward us on Routes 1 and 9, and air cavalry troops are flying to Khe Sanh in assault helicopters.

As word spreads around the base that help is coming, I can finally envisage an end to the long weeks I have lived here. Yet I remind myself that this isn't the time to let my guard down. I need to stay alert. It takes only one round to kill you, and more incoming will slam into our base before reinforcements arrive. It isn't over yet. I made it this far, so why get careless? I hope the relief forces hurry up and get here.

Bravo, Brave Company, March 30

These men must have been awake all night. Bravo Company is sending out another patrol. Bravo has lost more than fifty men and nearly three times as many wounded to enemy incoming; the bodies of twenty-five of its men still lie where they fell fighting at the site of last month's ambush. I couldn't sleep, aware that when the sun rises, I could be walking off the base onto the same patch of ground that twenty-five Marines didn't return from. Again I am on the perimeter to witness the men's departure. Khe Sanh's unique weather is upon us this morning, and the ground fog appears as moving walls of gaseous cottony white as it floats, suspended, along the ground. It reminds me of a haunted house movie scene.

Captain Kenneth Pipes will lead the patrol. All available artillery and mortars will be fired to explode on the sides and in front of the patrol. We will walk them out inside a steel box of shrapnel. The wall of shrapnel we explode in front of them will move at their pace, and at a distance of seventy-five yards. Their itinerary is mapped and broken down into sections; areas where fire might be needed are named apples, grapes, or oranges. Bravo can call by radio for more fire to either flank or ahead just by naming the proper fruit. Name the fruit, and the fire directional centers on base will know where to fire. Base artillery will put a wall of shrapnel beyond and behind the enemy bunkers, to keep the enemy from fleeing and also prevent North Vietnamese reinforcements from joining the upcoming battle. Bravo Company wants revenge on the North Vietnamese who killed their comrades.

I watch as Bravo lines up in battle formation. The men fix their bayonets. Outside the barbed wire, along the access road to the old coffee plantation, patches of ground fog slowly and silently drift away from the perimeter and out toward the enemy. The fog seems to be saying, "Just follow me."

Quietly, the patrol walks up to and follows the moving wall of fog. The fog and the Bravo men move along together at the same slow, determined pace. I have never seen man and weather in such unison. Today the fog is their friend; it is escorting them out and hiding them from the enemy's view. Bravo Company and the fog seem to have a common goal.

It is 0800. I run back to my gun pit to perform my duties as ammo man. I unwrap mortar rounds, remove safety pins, and stand by for any orders from the squad leader.

We begin firing. We explode a steel shrapnel wall for Bravo. More than likely, the enemy think it is just a regular shelling. They don't know that at that moment Bravo is walking toward them, concealed behind the moving wall of fog. The men of Bravo Company have only eight hundred meters to go before they meet the enemy to pay them back.

Our mortar barrel is glowing, because we are dropping round after round down the tube. As a round leaves our barrel, the next one is already posed to drop.

The fog conceals Bravo all the way up to the enemy bunkers and trench lines. Then it abruptly lifts, like a stage curtain rising to let the show begin.

I hear automatic weapons fire. The noise of the American M16s and the North Vietnamese AK-47s mingle. I have never heard so much gunfire at one time. The surprised North Vietnamese soldiers fire mortars into Bravo's ranks.

Bravo Company's radioman, the forward observer for artillery, and the forward observer for heavy mortars are killed outright. Captain Pipes takes a piece of shrapnel that lodges in his chest inches from his heart. He doesn't go down. He motions his men forward, right into the enemy trench lines and bunkers.

The men of Bravo Company leap into the enemy trenches with fixed bayonets, killing soldiers having breakfast as they wait for our barrage of artillery and mortar fire to lift.

Bravo fights for three hours. The men even use flamethrowers. They pay back the North Vietnamese Army. They kill more than a hundred enemy soldiers in close-quarter and hand-to-hand combat.

11: Seventy-Seven Days of Combat

Pegasus

In these last hours of March, allied units are starting out toward our base; it is called Operation Pegasus. Spearheading the relief force will be Marines. The 1st Marine Regiment and the 3d Marine Regiment will fight their way toward our base first. They will also protect the flanks of navy Seabees who will repair Route 9 bridges that were destroyed by the enemy in their efforts to cut supply lines to the base. The Marines are coming west from Dong Ha toward us.

Three brigades of the army's 1st Cavalry Division are coming—from Camp Evans in Da Nang and from Camp Hochmuth in Phu Bai. The army is coming in assault helicopters. The 4th Marine Regiment and part of the 1st ARVN Division are coming, too. Everybody and their mother is coming.

Relief Force

It is 0700 on April 1. We have been inside our defenses for seventy days, waiting to be attacked by North Vietnamese divisions, and we have endured enemy shelling through it all. My hearing saved me many times by giving me precious extra seconds to dive for cover. My vision is sharper. Now I can see the blurred outline of an enemy 122mm rocket in the air just before it strikes the base. When I can see the rocket, I know it won't strike close by, but the noise still frightens me.

I have acquired a dangerous habit: I shouldn't be looking up at all; I should be in a trench line, looking down, face in the dirt. Sometimes I admonish myself for this bad habit. I tell myself, "It's not over yet. It won't be until you're out of here."

M16

When time permits, between frequent fire missions at the mortar, we perform field maintenance on our own weapons. I keep my M16 and magazines spotless. I would be a fool if I didn't. When I clean my magazines, I remove the bullets to make sure no dirt has managed to cradle itself among them.

The plastic-stock M16 is lightweight and short compared to its predecessors, such as the M14 and M1 carbine, which had wooden stocks. The M16 barrel's housing and pistol grip give the weapon an avant-garde, space-age appearance compared to rifles issued by the military before it. The M16, manufactured by Colt Arms in Hartford, Connecticut, is easy to hump in the jungle. Some of the first ones manufactured were defective and jammed during firefights.

Before I enlisted in the Marines, I visited a friend who had just returned from Vietnam. Kenny O'Neil was a navy corpsman with the Marines and fought in these same mountain highlands of Vietnam. I walked over to his home on Elysian Avenue in Nyack, and as we sat on his porch that spring afternoon, he told me about a world I didn't know existed and couldn't imagine. He told me how he could still hear the shouts of "Corpsman up, corpsman up." He told me what he found when he went "up." He would often find wounded and dead Marines with their rifle's cleaning rod lying by their sides. Their M16s had jammed when needed most, during an ambush. The cleaning rod is one way to dislodge a bullet casing that is jammed in the rifle chamber.

Kenny kept saying, "Their M16s jammed. They didn't have a fighting chance." He would get all choked up and become depressed. I clean my M16 frequently because I can still see Kenny's face.

To quickly aim their rifle in darkness, some Marines stick a sliver of luminous tape directly on the sights. To prevent unnecessary rattling of the metal buckles on the rifle sling against the stock, some Marines wrap the buckles with tape. It eliminates the noise. Silence is part of stealth.

More Mail

My mother, ever the worrier, can be counted on to give me something to look forward to when mail arrives. She writes regularly, even though she has her hands full with my seven siblings. She keeps me informed of such important matters as who in the neighborhood isn't pulling weeds from their gardens, and which neighbor's grass is higher than she thinks it should be. She can get very upset if the price of a quart of milk goes up a couple of cents. She mentions in one of her letters that a cousin of hers shipped me a canned fruitcake. Her cousin figured that if it is in a can, it won't spoil in Vietnam's tropical heat. My mother writes that I can expect the fruitcake anytime. She doesn't know I have all the fruitcake I want because it comes in our C rations. I am sick of it. I haven't received the fruitcake in the mail yet; I think I know why. When supplies parachuted to us overshoot the drop zone and land outside our perimeter, they are blown up with base artillery so the enemy can't use our supplies. Whenever I think of my fruitcake's probable fate, a big grin comes over my face. I hate fruitcake.

Foxhole Dream

I am in a real bathroom. It has a beautiful porcelain sink and a sparkling-clean toilet. There is a bathtub and a shower with a new shower curtain. I am inside the shower. Here is a big bar of soap, and it is brand new. There is shampoo and toothpaste. I see neatly folded clean white towels. The shower is on. I have the nozzle pointed to spray directly on my face. The water temperature is just right. I had forgotten how wonderful a shower can be. I need this.

Oh, no, I am waking up. I was asleep and dreaming. I look for the shower nozzle as I wake, but I am lying here on my back. I am not in my shower anymore. It is raining in my face and on my clothing. I am cold now, and soaking wet.

Our Spirits

Morale is lifting because we know that help is on the way. We spend more time socializing. In the evenings we listen to radio broadcasts transmitted from North Vietnam. We gather in our gun pit with the radio resting on the circular sandbagged wall. The station broadcasts propaganda directed at American troops in South Vietnam. A woman named Hanoi Hannah tries to demoralize us with verbal unpleasantries and often broadcasts warnings to those of us at Khe Sanh that we will die here. Her propaganda makes us angry and gives us more resolve.

Because the relief force is on the way, these should be our last nights here. Our morale begins to soar. After listening to Hanoi Hannah, we tune in our American armed force's radio station. Several songs express our sentiments. One song is "We Gotta Get Out of This Place."

I worry when the volume is high on our radio. It is loud enough to mask the noise of a muzzle blast from an enemy gun; the volume could cost me those precious seconds that I need to take cover. Something as simple as the volume button on a radio can cost you your life. Still, I don't say anything, because I don't want to put a damper on the festivities.

We are so happy with thoughts of getting out of here that we dance. Our gun pit is the dance floor. We are careful not to bump into our mortar when we dance; its barrel is aimed skyward, sight leveled, waiting to be fired. We laugh uncontrollably as we dance. Crisp, clacking sounds can be heard as loose fiberglass panels in our flak jackets smack together. This is how we pass our time during what we believe to be our last nights here.

Too Quiet

It is April 9, almost sunset. Something very strange happened; actually it is what didn't happen that is strange. All day long the enemy have not fired one shell into our base, not one.

In the darkness at West Dickens, awake and scanning our lines for the long-awaited enemy soldiers who never come, I wonder why the enemy didn't fire on us at all this day. Perhaps they are gone.

April 10 Morning

Now I know the real feeling of springtime. I think I will get to live life after all. The morning sunrise looks more beautiful than ever before. I am out and away from my foxhole, standing by strands of barbed wire, looking off to the east, inhaling deep breaths of the beautiful valley air. I even feel like spring.

I am not the only one. Around me, other Marines are out of their trenches, foxholes, and bunkers seemingly doing the same thing: They are savoring that same spring feeling. The sun, warming my body, feels good.

More Incoming

The enemy have opened fire again. Maybe they didn't fire yesterday because they wanted to clean their weapons, or maybe they just wanted to rest. I am tired of people trying to kill me.

April 13 Evening

We get word that friendly forces will be here in the morning. Along with the news heralding their pending arrival is additional information that I don't care to hear. When the relief force arrives, we will be leaving, on foot. Orders are issued. At first light tomorrow, we are to saddle up and bring only what is necessary to survive in the jungle for several days. We are to destroy any remaining items that can be useful to our enemy, especially food. We are to destroy our bunkers.

I am selective, packing the items I will need. Weight is a determining factor. We will take our mortar with us—disassembled. As an ammo man, it is my job to carry part of the weapon. I will be carrying the base plate—the steel outer ring that rests on the ground into which the barrel is seated for firing. The base plate is heavy. I will also be carrying several high-explosive 81mm mortar rounds.

Before I destroy my cache of C rations, I sort them and select several cans for food to eat while in the jungle. I put these to one side. Outside my foxhole, I place canteens, poncho, poncho liner, utility belt, bayonet, M16, ammunition clips, grenades, first-aid kit, several bottles of insect repellent, and all my cigarettes. That is all I am taking with me. My guitar, stored in another unused foxhole, was blown up. I would have left it here, anyway.

It is time to destroy the C rations that I can't carry with me. I stab my cans of discarded C rations with my bayonet so they will spoil and give insects and the fat Khe Sanh rats easy access to their contents. As I stab each can, I place it in a pile. In the morning I will throw them into my foxhole for burial.

I will carry out the second order, pertaining to the destruction of my foxhole, in the morning. It will be my last act before saddling up with all my gear. I will need my foxhole tonight for protection against incoming enemy shells.

Last Night at Khe Sanh

None of us sleeps well. We are troubled, and we all wonder whether we could possibly be hit by an incoming round on this, our last night here. I also wonder what will happen in the morning when we leave the perimeter. What will we find out there? Whom will we find out there?

The fat Khe Sanh rats must know we are leaving. They are out en-masse tonight. It might be the scent from the cans of rations that we opened to let spoil. It might just be that they know we are leaving and they will soon have the outpost to themselves.

I count my blessings on this last night. I am fortunate not to be wounded or dead. I am also fortunate that I wasn't stationed on the nearby hills. I don't know if I could have survived on Hill 861 or Hill 881S. I didn't have to stay awake all night, as those men did. I could catch an hour of sleep here and there. I didn't have to fight in hand-to-hand combat, as they did. I didn't have to look my enemy straight in the eye.

Good-bye, West Dickens, April 14

The sun is up, but we can't leave yet because the relief forces aren't all in place. I am not destroying West Dickens until the last moment. I might need it for ducking enemy shells. I make coffee, then write a final letter home from Khe Sanh and stick it in my pocket.

I hear helicopter engines. The noise is coming from the east, way out in the valley. I hear the sound the rotor blades make as they smack the air to keep the helicopter aloft. Elements of the relief force are approaching. I leap from West Dickens, coffee still in hand, for a better view. The helicopters belong to the army air cavalry.

I admire the courage of the soldiers inside those metal birds, com-ing to face the unknown. They are carrying weapons locked and loaded, ready for bear. They are camouflaged for jungle stealth, and the smokers are probably nervously sucking a drag on a final cigarette before landing. These are brave men, flying to this infamous, storied place. They are probably expecting the worst. But it's really all over.

The formation of choppers descends, and the first one I see land-ing couldn't have chosen a worst spot. There is no way we can warn the pilot from this distance. My worst fears come true. There is an explosion just yards away from the chopper's landing skids. A soldier is hurt. I see him go down. It looks like the explosion of an enemy 61mm mortar round.

Suddenly there is chaos on the landing zone (LZ). I watch as other air cavalry soldiers go to aid the wounded soldier. He got it literally the moment he set foot on Khe Sanh. I curse the enemy for him. The enemy gunner hasn't fired a second round at them yet. Pilots of the choppers following this first aircraft and about to land see this, so they leapfrog their aircraft away from that landing spot and seek their own LZs nearby.

I return to my foxhole, sit on its roof, and watch as more and more helicopters come over the horizon. After seventy-seven days, they are finally here.

A jeep is coming toward me. It has no bullet or shrapnel holes, so it can't be one of ours. Our jeeps all have battle damage: holes, flat tires, and broken windshields. The jeep pulls up right in front of West Dickens. Riding in the jeep is an army officer and his driver. Army? The overland relief force has arrived.

The jeep stops in front of me, and the driver turns off the engine. Both men stare at me in silence. After a long moment, the army officer finally speaks. "Are you okay?" What a stupid question. "Yeah, I'm fine. Thanks for coming. Listen, I've got to go outside the wire this morning. We're going on patrol for a couple of days. That's our orders. Would you please mail this letter for me if you get the chance?" I reach into my pocket and pull out the letter I wrote earlier and hand it to the officer. They stare at me in disbelief. "Are you sure you're okay?"

It occurs to me why they are acting strange. They are looking around and taking in the sights: wrecked helicopters and airplanes, a blown ammo dump, shrapnel carpeting the entire area, burned sandbags, craters, trench lines, foxholes, thousands of discarded safety pins pulled from mortar rounds, my ripped and stained jungle clothing, the fiberglass panels protruding from my flak jacket. They are seeing for the first time what I have been looking at for months: destruction.

I answer his question again; I assure him I am okay. I tell him there might be other Marines in my section who would like to mail letters also. Would he ask around? He assures me he will. The driver starts the jeep. Before they drive off, they both take one long final look at me and my foxhole.

As lead elements of the relief force arrive, I know I will be leaving soon. I decide to destroy West Dickens. I stand back from my foxhole and take a last look at my very lucky place in the ground. What memories. The words of that orientation officer flash through my mind once again. "Dig in, dig in now!"

The first thing I do is throw the pile of discarded C-ration cans into the front of the hole. Then I push the row of sandbags, aligned on the parapet, into the front section. I stand on the roof of the back section, remove the sandbags one by one, and throw them into the open front part to fill it. Then I discard the layer of wooden pallets. I stare into the now unroofed back section and remember those terrifying moments when I was cringing in there as the ammo dump blew up, and I recall the cigarette filters we inserted into our ears to muffle the terrifying sounds of the explosions. It seems like years ago. I cave in the dirt walls of the back section with a shovel, then remove my yellow street sign. I throw the West Dickens Avenue sign into the nearly filled front portion of my hole.

The destruction of my foxhole is complete, but I have one more thing to do. I remove one of my two dog tags from the chain around my neck. I intend to drop it on the road as we walk off the base, because I want somebody, someday, years from now, to find it. I want somebody to know that I was here and that Khe Sanh was my home. Maybe someday, someone will find a metal dog tag here and will read: "Corbett, John A., USMC, 2321157, Caucasian, Blood type O."

My dog tags are not the same type that were issued to soldiers before me. Mine don't have a notch. The old dog tags had a notch that enabled fellow soldiers to wedge the dog tag between your teeth if you were killed in action. That way, all someone had to do to identify your body at a later date was to open your mouth. My dog tags are smooth edged all the way around.

Saddle Up

My field gear is ready. I am bringing only three C-ration meals. I have filled my two canteens. My poncho and poncho liner are folded and in my haversack, fastened to my rigid fiberglass backboard. I will carry one of my canteens in its canvas cover, attached to my belt. On this wide adjustable utility belt, I will also carry my bayonet in its rigid sheath. I tie two high-explosive mortar rounds to the backboard and place two smooth-surfaced hand grenades, nicknamed baseballs, in my haversack, at the very top, for over-the-shoulder easy access. My two remaining grenades will be in a more accessible place than my haversack; I insert them in the pockets of a magazine bandoleer that I can sling over my shoulder. I put cigarettes and several plastic squeeze bottles of insect repellent in my haversack. I check the contents of my first-aid kit and attach it to my belt. My magazines are filled and inserted into individual compartments in another cloth bandoleer. I don't sling my M16 over my shoulder; I will carry it at the ready. I make certain I have heat tabs in my pockets to warm my food.

Our 81mm Mortar

As I carry the base plate of our mortar, I feel as though I am carrying a big steel doughnut.

Another squad member carries the inner part of the base plate, which is solid steel and has a rope handle. The mortar's metal bipod legs are carried by another man, and the barrel is carried by yet another. The mortar's leveling sight is boxed and carried by one man, and another carries the barber poles: the red-and-white aiming stakes by which the mortar's gun sight is oriented.

I knew when I joined the Marine Corps that it wouldn't be easy, but I didn't know how right I was. I never thought I would be humping a chunk of steel around the jungle. I quickly learn the best way to carry the outer ring: slip my arm through it and let it rest on my shoulder. The thick fabric of my flak jacket lessens the pain inflicted by its weight. Also, carrying it suspended from my shoulder gives me use of both hands so I can fire my rifle.

My backpack is so heavy that I ask another Marine to hoist it onto my back while I slip my arms through the shoulder straps.

Walking Off

We form two columns and each space ourselves from the Marine directly in front of us. We will remain in this formation until we enter the jungle. We will walk west-southwest down the length of the base's dirt road first, because we are on the eastern perimeter.

There is shouting and verbal spars, which are meant to shape up our formation and establish some semblance of order. There are repeated shouts: "Spread out. One round will get you all."

Soon we are equally spaced from the Marine to our front, rear, and flank. I feel the weight of my gear, and I haven't gone anywhere yet. In formation, I see my comrades in numbers for the first time. Until now, because we have occupied trenches, bunkers, and foxholes, they have been visible only a few at a time. Everybody has red skin. Khe Sanh isn't just in our minds; it is in our bodies. Our skin has absorbed the valley's fine red volcanic soil.

Most of the men I see are strangers. Although they are my comrades, I don't recognize many, other than the members of our mortar section. All the men I see are worn out. They have tattered and torn clothing, just as I do. There are a few "new guy" replacements; I can tell by their clothing and flak jackets, which are reasonably clean and unfaded. All of us, even the newer Marines, have the "thousand-yard stare": eyes glazed and brain numb. It is an indication that we have seen too much combat. Some Marines, including me, have body sores due to the lack of bathing facilities.

Carrying all this weight is the first exercise I have had in months. I didn't exercise daily, as some Marines did. I didn't jump out of my foxhole each morning and give the valley fifty push-ups. I think I am going to regret it.

Everyone I see is implementing the learned survival mechanism of constantly scanning his surroundings, looking for that depression in the ground, or the nearest crater to dive into, when that next round comes screeching in. I am, too.

We are leaving. We are walking slowly. I take the dog tag from my pocket and drop it on the dirt road and kick some dirt over it.

My gear is heavier than that of the other Marines, because I am humping the mortar's base plate. Here I am in Vietnam, in their lunar new year of the monkey, on my way to see the dragon, feeling more like a pack mule than a combat Marine.

I walk along the road to our base's western perimeter. I see a priest up ahead with a stole around his neck and a book in his hand, which must be a Bible. The Marines, in formation, each pause for a second as they pass him. Each speaks just a few quick words. The priest is repeatedly making the sign of the cross with his outstretched arm, blessing everybody and everything near him. Am I coming back from this patrol?

I remember when I boarded the airplane to Vietnam, there was a man at the bottom of the plane's rollaway staircase handing out pocket-sized battlefield Bibles. Everybody took one but me. If there is a God, I don't believe he goes to war.

Into the Bush

My part of the column is off the base. We walk across some grass that is over my boot tops and finally enter the jungle growth. As I walk off the base, which is a fixed target for enemy guns, I feel as if I am born again.

Under the jungle canopy, we immediately come onto a well-worn path. We follow it for twenty minutes, being very quiet, before coming upon a downed helicopter. It is a Marine chopper, a CH-53. Downed helicopters have their own mystique about them. The finder's mind starts to ask questions. "When was it shot down?" "Did the crew get out okay?" "Was the crew plucked from enemy hands by another helicopter crew just in the nick of time?" "Was the crew taken prisoner?"

The airframe appears intact. The helicopter might have been mechanically disabled by enemy fire and had to land. It was maneuvered to land upright on its landing gear. It has been here for a while. Jungle grass and weeds have grown up around its wheels and cling to them.

As we proceed silently down the trail, the jungle landscape changes drastically. It has been landscaped by air strikes. Craters are all over the place; many are overlapping circles.

As we proceed slowly—and hyperalert—still close to the outskirts of the base, I hear explosions. Incoming is striking our combat base again.

Command Change

Two days ago, our 26th Marine Regiment commander, Col. David Lownds, was replaced. He did his job; he kept the base from the enemy.

Sometimes being in the lower ranks has its advantages. If the base had been overrun by the enemy, they would have blamed him, not me. Our new regimental commander is Col. Bruce Meyers.

Last night, the 3d Battalion of my regiment, commanded by Lt. Col. John C. Studt, went out to position itself for a daylight attack on Hill 881N. Intense artillery fire from allied guns is presently softening up the enemy's fortifications there. An officer who observed them setting out for their objective this morning is concerned about the physical condition of the men, because they have been confined to living in foxholes and trenches for three months, eating only canned rations, and often short of water. He shouldn't be as concerned about their physical condition as their mental condition.

The 3d Battalion is making contact, and some of the enemy soldiers, bombed from their bunkers by the preparatory artillery fire, flee into the open. The men chase the enemy with fixed bayonets and can't be stopped. The frustration of being on the receiving end of enemy guns for nearly three months is finally vented on the North Vietnamese. The Marines are storming the hilltop and killing anyone in their way.

We are on a jungle path and blend in with the foliage. I can see only three or four Marines to my front and three or four to my rear. We walk slowly, our rifles at the ready. Our thumbs are on the safety switch, ready to select semiautomatic or full-automatic fire. I have my safety off. My rifle's thumb selector switch is on semiautomatic. We are moving slowly and silently, watching where we step, so as not to snap a twig and make noise. We constantly turn our heads, looking from one side of the trail to the other, scanning with our eyes, trying to detect anything that seems out of place. The enemy might be able to see us, but we are so quiet that they definitely can't hear us.

Suddenly our column stops. I look ahead and see the Marine in front of me receiving a whispered message from the Marine ahead of him. The man in front of me motions me forward. Maybe something has been spotted up ahead. I slowly approach and our helmets touch as he whispers in my ear. "Happy Easter! Pass it on."

I wave to the Marine behind me to come forward for the message. I whisper "Happy Easter" in his ear and tell him to pass it on. I didn't even know what day of the week it was. I didn't know today was a Sunday, let alone Easter Sunday. I recall Easter Sundays past, all those chocolate-rabbit Sundays of my childhood. My parents got us four boys new suits, complete with fedoras, to wear to church. I remember those wonderful holiday meals of turkey and ham. I wish I could eat one now. I recall woven Easter baskets wrapped in colorful, see-through cellophane, with all the goodies inside.

I wish no one had told me it was Easter Sunday. It is hard to bring my thoughts back to the business at hand. This is not an Easter egg hunt, and we are not out here looking for the Easter bunny. If we find anything, it won't be Easter eggs; it will be booby traps. Finding an egg would be nice. I haven't eaten one since the mess hall was blown up nearly three months ago.

Later

Looking forward, up the trail, I see a massive swarm of insects. I watch as they engulf the Marine in front of me. The swarm continues down the trail toward me. I am next! I have never seen the likes of this before. The insects are buzzing like bees, though these bugs are smaller. The Marine up front, engulfed in the swarm, hasn't yelped as though he has been stung, so I guess the insects are harmless. They look like horseflies, though they are not. They are aggressive, and I need to think quickly. I don't want to be covered with insect bites. I sink to my knees, drop the mortar base plate from my shoulder, and set my M16 on the ground. I slip off my backpack and quickly remove and unfold my poncho. "Do what I'm doing!" I tell the Marine behind me, the next one who will be swarmed. I don't wait to see if he follows my example. I wrap myself in the poncho and squat low to the ground. My timing is good. The insects swarm over my poncho, making sounds like the patter of large raindrops. There are thousands of patters. This is a giant swarm.

Though I am completely wrapped in my poncho and can't see, the frequency of the bug strikes on my poncho finally tapers off. It is now safe for me to unwrap myself. I see the swarm passing over the Marine behind me. He is following my example, covering himself with his poncho for protection. The swarm passes over him and he unwraps, too. "Good thinking, Jack," he says as he emerges. The way things are starting out, this is definitely going to be an Easter Sunday to remember.

Bodies

I think the NVA soldier has been dead for a couple of days. He is lying on the trail wearing his helmet. The hats worn by the NVA resemble the hat I saw Ramar of the Jungle wear on television when I was a kid. Jungle Jim wore one, too.

The enemy soldier is lying on his back, and there is dried blood around his waist. As I stand over him, I wonder what weapon caused his death. His body isn't mangled, and his clothing has no noticeable holes. The chin strap holds his jungle hat squarely and firmly in position, as if he were standing erect and alive. Maybe it was the concussion from one of the B-52 bombs that killed him. Maybe it was a small piece of shrapnel that entered at high velocity. Maybe he has tiny steel arrows inside him from an exploded beehive artillery round. Whatever it was, he is dead. He is in uniform and wearing a canvas web belt with a square chrome buckle. I don't think it is wise to root through his canvas backpack looking for souvenirs. His backpack might be booby-trapped. If I remove his belt for a souvenir, I will disturb his body too much. I really want his belt buckle, which looks like silver and has the imprint of the Communist star, but I am leery of cutting the buckle away from his canvas belt. I have read about how the Japanese in World War II booby-trapped bodies of their dead comrades, anticipating that Marines such as I would search them for souvenirs. I will just be careful. Gently, I cut the metal buckle from his canvas belt with my bayonet. The Marine behind me watches. "Jack, I think you've lost it." I *have* lost it. I remove a heat tab from my pocket, light it, and sterilize the buckle by holding it over the flame.

The farther we walk along the path, the more craters there are in the landscape around us. I can tell what kind of bomb made each crater by its size. The widest and deepest craters were made by 2,000-pound bombs dropped from B-52 bombers, the next largest by 1,000-pounders, the next by 750-pound bombs, then 500-pounders. The smaller gouges in the ground are from artillery rounds, and smaller yet are the depressions made by 81mm mortar rounds. The smallest scars are from the 61mm mortars.

As we walk along the cratered landscape, I come upon a long section of wire lying on the ground. As I pull it out of the soil, I discover that the wire is longer than I thought, but I continue to rip it up from the dirt, letting it lead me to its point of origin. I follow it for thirty feet as it leads me off the trail toward a large crater. The crater has been made by a 500-pound bomb, probably dropped by a jet. Around the crater is a bank of soft soil gouged from the earth by the detonated bomb. In the pile of soil I spot the half-buried barrel of an enemy 61mm mortar and conclude that the jet dropped its bomb on target, directly onto the enemy mortar and its gun crew. There is no sign of the enemy crew. They were probably blown to pieces by the explosion. Scattered on the ground around the crater are their mortar rounds. I pick up the nearest mortar round and examine its markings. It was manufactured by the Chinese. Also scattered on the ground are about a dozen Chinese Communist (chicom) grenades. The lightweight grenades have a cap on top of the fat end that houses the explosives; they also have handles to facilitate throwing. The cap, which protects the grenade's point-detonating pin, is attached by a short piece of string; removing the pin activates the grenade for throwing. As I pick up one of the enemy grenades and pull off its cap, the Marines near me scatter in all directions. One of them shouts, "Corbett, you're crazy," as he runs away from me and the grenade. After they reach cover, I gently replace the cap. I am not crazy, just curious.

I pull on the barrel of the 61mm mortar and take it from the soil. As I do, I wonder if this was the gun, now minus its crew, that was responsible for my friend Mark's death. I hope it is. Now I wonder if it is the same gun that fired that mortar round at me the time I was on the perimeter taking pictures. I hope it is.

Gunfire

We have been in the jungle surrounding the combat base for several hours and as yet have had no contact with the enemy. We are becoming a little more at ease. We are not as cautious about making noise as we were when we first left the combat base. "BANG!" I hit the ground. It is a rifle shot. Then I scramble for cover, my M16 at the ready. Thirty seconds go by and no more gunfire follows the rifle shot. More gunfire would signal that a firefight with the enemy is under way. That is not the case. A Marine ahead of me on the trail accidentally discharged his rifle. Therefore, all our efforts to sneak up on the enemy are for naught. If they are here, they know we are here. If they had a doorbell, we just rang it. Although the rifle shot couldn't have come at a worse time, I am not angry with the Marine, because it could have happened to any one of us.

Afternoon

We are walking through an area known as Leech Valley, where the resident leeches have no mercy. A Marine had a leech enter his trousers and crawl halfway into his penis. I brush several off my hands and lower arms before a man alongside me says brushing them off is like smacking a yellowjacket or a wasp that just stung me; the stinger remains embedded. If I just brush away the soft leech, its head will come off and remain under my skin and cause an infection. He says the way to completely get rid of a leech is to hold a lit match or a lighted cigarette to its tail; the leech will pull its head back out from underneath the skin and leave.

My canteens are empty. I haven't rationed my water. As we made our way into the jungle, when I felt like a drink, I drank as if there were a reservoir just up the trail. What water I couldn't swallow I let spill out of my mouth and run down my chest. My flak jacket holds the heat, so the water running down my chest refreshed me. Taking big swigs also lightened my load.

I sweat profusely in the rain forest. My clothes are saturated. I look at my arms and can't see a dry patch of skin. I am not sweating beads of sweat, I am sweating sheets of water. Garments easily rot in this climate from the combination of sweat and salt from one's body. When I let my arm hang straight at my side, the sweat flows down it and drips off my fingertips.

It is easy to succumb to heat stoke here, and I am out of water on this, my first afternoon patrol in the jungle, at the hottest time of the day. I am dizzy from the sun and lack of water. There is a small stream just ahead. I can see that it is only inches deep, but it looks crystal clear. I am down on my belly at its edge, drinking.

I stand up and vomit. My stomach has spasms. The stream has been fouled by the decaying bodies of our enemy, killed by bombs dropped from our jets.

I am more thirsty now. There is a large puddle of stagnant brownish water. I never knew that thirst could be so powerful. I submerge my canteen in the puddle. Unfortunately, Leech Valley lives up to its name and leeches flow with the water into my canteen. I use my thumbs as sentinels at the canteen's spout to shoo them away. Big gulps of puddle water quench my thirst. This time I don't vomit.

Going for a Swim

We come upon a large crater filled with water. Its size indicates it was blown out by a large bomb from a Boeing B-52. The crater is fed by a small stream, and the water looks crystal clear. I feel as though I have found an oasis. Our column has halted, so I fill my canteens first. None of us has had a bath in months, so a few of us decide to take a swim. I strip and jump in. The water is simultaneously cleansing and cooling. Each of us takes a turn standing guard, watching for the enemy, while the others swim. I stand guard nude as I hold my M16. I laugh at myself, imagining what the enemy would think if they came upon a naked Marine in the jungle.

Word is passed along our column that we are to camouflage. As we gather greenery from the side of the trail, we find that in this region of fertile coffee plantations, some farmer planted more than just coffee beans. We are in a crop of *Cannabis sativa*. In Asia, it is grown and used for medicine. We are all smiling as we camouflage ourselves with marijuana. Several Marines get carried away and insert as many cuttings as they can into the slits of their helmet covers. One Marine jokes that he will wear his marijuana camouflage until the hot tropical sun dries it enough to be smoked. As for me, I look like a tree with too many branches. So far I have a souvenir, I have taken a swim, and I am camouflaged in pot—three for three.

My column has probed out from the base in a fortunate direction, west. So far there have been no enemy to offer resistance. Other platoons and squads from the three battalions of my regiment haven't been as lucky.

We slowly advance onto ground that for the last three months has been held by the North Vietnamese Army. We come upon empty enemy trenches. I notice some differences between their trenches and ours. Theirs are shallower and deep enough for the occupant to be protected only up to his hips. Our trenches are deeper; we can stand upright and still be completely below ground level.

It is my first night away from West Dickens. Tonight I will be sleeping in enemy territory. Sentinels are posted, and a circular defensive perimeter is established. I am not chosen to stand guard, so I will have a chance to sleep—on the ground circled by Marines on watch for the enemy during the night. I wrap myself in my poncho to ward off insects and protect against a possible tropical rain shower. I hear faint noises of incoming rounds exploding onto the distant combat base. I am exhausted from carrying heavy combat gear all day. Before sleep comes, my last thoughts are of past Easter Sundays. Going to sleep is no problem. I am so tired that if the enemy came I wouldn't hear them.

It is first light. No enemy came last night. I open my eyes to find myself still tightly wrapped in my poncho as if it were a cocoon. I am in the same position as when I fell asleep. I haven't tossed, turned, or moved at all during the night, a sign that I was deeply tired. In the early-morning light I see what appears to be two large rocks lying on the ground near my face. I didn't see them last night. Still wrapped in my poncho, I reel back in fright, trying to rise to my feet. They are not rocks. They are two heads. The faces of both are directed at me. Both heads have close-cropped black hair. They are the heads of two enemy soldiers. They have been cleanly severed, and their torsos are not in sight. I make it to my feet, still in shock. I think these two enemy soldiers are casualties of a bomb we call a daisy cutter. It strikes the ground, then rises several feet and explodes to release its shrapnel at the height of the upper torso. I unwrap my poncho and move several feet away, then I sit down and boil water with a heat tab. I will have my morning coffee with the two North Vietnamese; I would eat, but I am not hungry.

"Saddle up, saddle up." The order is passed from one man to another. We are on the jungle trail again. The field map is sectioned into parcels by grid lines that form boxes. It breaks down the terrain into grid squares. It shows us that we have progressed straight from the combat base on a west-southwest heading, equidistant from Hills 689 and 471, and are now located between two small settlements. The village of Xom Ta Can is to the north and Chau Lang Chanh is to the south. Whatever structures once existed in these small villages are no longer, and the people who lived here are gone.

Any villagers who didn't flee while they had the chance are probably dead, casualties of bombs dropped by planes or artillery and mortar fire from our Khe Sanh base and Camp Carroll and the Rockpile. Why people would choose to live in Leech Valley surrounded by leeches, I don't understand.

On our second day in enemy territory, I realize that we are walking in a miles-long semicircle that will, in a day or two, return us to the base.

Return to Base

Through the jungle growth I see a clearing up ahead, illuminated by sunshine, where my column will shortly enter. It is the cleared, sunlit patches of ground that are the fringes of the combat base itself. The sunlit area up ahead is in contrast to the darker ground we are walking on. We are under triple-canopy foliage. In most places the sunlight can't penetrate to the jungle floor. It is shady to the point of darkness. The sunlit area I see up ahead, at the southwest corner of the base perimeter, is the same patch of boot-high grass that I trod through several days ago to go on this patrol.

As we emerge I hear and see aircraft. The sky is alive with helicopters and C-123 and C-130 cargo planes. Each airplane, in turn, is quickly landing and filling up with groups of Marines who have mustered to await evacuation. They came out of the jungle before us. The planes spend little time on the airstrip; they quickly taxi to the waiting Marines but don't come to a full stop. Their loading ramps lower and Marines run up into the cargo bays. I see several planes begin their takeoff rolls with Marines following on the run, chasing the still lowered and unclosed ramps.

As we come out of the jungle and walk onto the sunlit grass, the column I have been part of breaks into smaller groups of men. My squad positions itself high on the grass at the edge of the base perimeter. From where I am standing in the grass, just yards out from the tree line, I can look over into the combat base. The jungle is to my back and due west. As I gaze into the base, I feel tremendous apprehension. I don't want to get any closer. I am frightened at the prospect of having to spend another night on this cratered, targeted outpost, where I have been bombed night and day.

My apprehension at having to reenter is not necessary. I am leaving, too. Helicopters—twin-rotor Sea Knights—hover above the ground to the north, evacuating squads of Marines who have gathered and are huddled in the grass, as we are, outside of but along the western perimeter of the combat base. One at a time, the helicopters fly at us at a high and determined speed. As one settles down to load troops, another one approaches, leapfrogs, then lands to load, too.

Adrenaline flowing, I anxiously wait with my squad until our turn comes. It shouldn't be long now. The brave chopper pilots and their Sea Knight helicopters have come to get us out of Khe Sanh.

Not Now!

The enemy start to fire 82mm mortar rounds at us. Their fire strikes and explodes closest to my huddled squad. It seems, ironically, that the NVA mortar squad has targeted us, its counterparts. I am cursing loudly. Could I die here moments before my opportunity to leave?

We are on our bellies in the grass, cringing. There is no hole or crater to crawl into. I watch as the mortar rounds explode. Each impact comes closer and closer. The enemy gunners are "walking" their mortar rounds toward us—adjusting their gun elevation with each fired round until they reach their target—as we just lie here. There is nothing we can do.

A round explodes in the grass near us. I notice a difference in the sound of the explosion. The grass muffles the noise. It is not the harsh-sounding blast that I am accustomed to. It is not the same sound that a mortar round makes when it explodes on the hardpan soil of the combat base. The sound doesn't matter, though. The mortar round is still capable of killing or wounding.

I feel as though I am lying here naked. There is no place to hide. I am shocked by the reality of what is happening. The possibility of getting killed in my last minutes at Khe Sanh is very real.

The helicopter pilots are evacuating us as fast as they can. There are three other groups of Marines about twenty-five yards apart from one another, lying in the grass to the north of us and along the western perimeter of the combat base. They will be evacuated before our turn comes. They are not under fire. We are running out of time. It will take longer for our turn to come than it will take the enemy gunners to walk their mortar rounds to us and explode them in our midst.

As I lie in the grass, I raise my head to watch a chopper hover over the group of Marines farthest from us. It is their turn. I am beginning to lose hope of leaving here in one piece. The pilot of the helicopter surely sees that our squad is under fire. The explosions, the smoke, and the dirt blown up from the mortar rounds are easily visible to him. We are so close, yet so far away.

The rescue chopper suddenly aborts its descent to the far group of Marines. It points its nose in our direction and flies toward us, its twin rotors loudly slapping the air. I see the helicopter's door gunner; his weapon is at the ready, protruding from the window. As the helicopter approaches us, the door gunner leans far out of his window. He motions to us, frantically moving his arms, beckoning us to rise and approach his aircraft. This aircrew is either brave or nuts. They could have chosen to evacuate the groups of Marines not under fire. Nobody would have blamed them; it wasn't my squad's turn yet. But they chose to rescue us instead.

We rise from the grass, then run to the hovering chopper. Its landing gear has not even settled fully to the ground. Someone shouts loud enough to be heard over the noise of the roaring engines: "Let's get the hell out of here!"

It sounds like a good idea to me. Though weighted down by all my combat gear, I never felt so light. I am at my top running speed as an enemy mortar round strikes and explodes nearby. I am under the helicopter's whirling blades. There are shouts from Marines behind me. I can hear them over the noise of the thunderous engines. I am so close I can feel the engine heat. I can see the hot exhaust creating blurs in the air, distorting my vision. I glance over my shoulder and quickly learn what the shouting is about. A Marine is down. He has been wounded by that last mortar round.

I am steps away from a ride out of this place, and a Marine gets wounded. The door gunner is screaming at me to run up the ramp of the helicopter and into the belly of his metal bird. I can't leave yet. We must go to the aid of the Marine who just hit the ground. I turn to go back, resigned to being at Khe Sanh for a couple minutes longer. I run back to the Marine, who is down in the grass. Suddenly two other Marines run up from behind the downed Marine. Each one grabs an arm and yanks him to his feet. He isn't wounded at all. He just tripped and fell!

We all dash to the still waiting chopper, run up the ramp, and sit on the floor, our backs against the metal walls. The door gunner is shouting to the pilot. "Go, go, go!" His words sound sweet in my ears.

The helicopter climbs for altitude in long, circular turns within the airspace immediately above the combat base. When the pilot has taken our Sea Knight as high in the sky as it is designed for, he will fly from the Khe Sanh plateau. I envision those enemy antiaircraft emplacements that surrounded the base perimeter and shot at our supply planes and choppers. I wonder if any are still there. It doesn't take much to shoot a helicopter out of the sky. In the tightness of the chopper's ascending turns, there is a slight rocking motion. I can feel it while sitting on the floor, and I can see it by looking at the Marines next to and across from me. Our heads gently sway back and forth and to and from one another.

Each of us is silent, in deep thought and in fear. No one wants to get shot down after surviving three months at Khe Sanh. The chopper is flying straight now. The pilot has set his course. We are hopefully high enough and out of range of enemy antiaircraft guns. We are still silent. We think of distance now. Have we flown out and away from Khe Sanh yet? None of us is standing. I am looking out of the window across from me.

Suddenly there is cheering. Cheers for being out and away from Khe Sanh. Cheers for the brave chopper pilot and his crew who came to our rescue under fire.

I am flying away from Khe Sanh! I remember the inscription that was printed on Khe Sanh's makeshift air tower, the words I saw moments after arriving at the base: "WELCOME TO KHE SANH." I have lived here more than three months. Seventy-seven days of that time, the enemy tried to kill me. I feel much older now. I feel older now than my father. I feel older now than my father's father. In fact, I feel like an old, old man. I have left my youth in Khe Sanh.

We are flying to somewhere else in South Vietnam. I still have ten months left to serve before I see America again.

12: Back to the Jungle

We have had a week's rest. The helicopter that flew us out of Khe Sanh took us to an army base called Wunder Beach. There the army positioned us on the outermost perimeters—closest to the enemy. We were mortared by the Viet Cong. I noticed when the incoming exploded that it sounded different from that in Khe Sanh. It was a muffled sound, even softer to the eardrums than when it impacts on grass. At Wunder Beach, I broke into an army officer's hooch and stole a bottle of Chivas Regal and got my squad drunk.

Now we are on an operation somewhere in the jungle west of Quang Tri near a river named Cua Viet. The names of these tiny villages I pass by or walk through do not matter. It is not as if I am a tourist. There are no postcards here. If there were postcards, what would I write on them? "Hi, having fun in the jungle somewhere near the Cua Viet River. Wish you were here." It is just another river. It is just another village where people live who don't care if we live or die on their doorsteps or in their farm fields. It is just another rice paddy with knee-deep water and a muddy bottom.

I walk out from the concealment of a tree line. We walk in places where water buffalo are smart enough not to go. The tree line at least provided some concealment. This is not a smart move. We are in the open, visible, and in danger. The enemy can easily spot us, and there is no place to seek cover from an ambush. As I walk up a slight rise, I have a pleasant thought: After Khe Sanh, the ten months remaining of my tour in Vietnam will be a piece of cake.

It is very hot. I need a drink from my canteen. My water is flavored with Kool-Aid to mask the natural bad taste of Vietnam's water. The column pauses briefly. At the crest of a slight ridgeline, I sit down for a few minutes. I need this break. I unscrew the black plastic top from my canteen and let it dangle on the chain that attaches it. Tilting my head back, I raise the canteen to my mouth and guzzle. I think about how nice it is to be out of range of enemy artillery.

"BAM, BAM, BAM!"

A Marine officer of Delta Company, the company I am on patrol with, was yards ahead of me. Unbeknownst to him or me, he will be a published author someday. He will write about what happens next. He tells it best.

"Ernie"

"We are bracketed by four of our artillery fire bases. They are firing on our next objective, a tree line near the Cua Viet River. The colonel and the S3 [Operations and Planning] move ahead to watch the prep fires. Then . . . Bang! I land in my hole. Bang! A guy's on top of me. Dirt is blowing in my open mouth and nose. I had opened my mouth to balance the concussion of the explosions. I taste dirt and smell sulfur from the arty [artillery] rounds. My eardrums are numb . . . I'm dead. I knew it, goddamn it, I . . . knew it. Close to us a guy is screaming his screams of oncoming death. He's being taken out slow. I hear Crazy Doc yelling, 'Somebody check those guys.' 'I'll check them,' one of my clerks yells from nearby. . . . 'You OK, Captain?' the guy on top of me asks. He's wrapped around me like a mink stole . . . and he's looking into my face. 'Yeah,' I say. He jumps out of the hole and is gone. I never see him again.

"As I stand up, I notice my clerk standing between the S-4 [Logistics and Supply] and a radio operator. They are 10 feet away. The

S-4 is laid out on his back, gurgling sounds are coming out of him. The radio operator is curled up and on his left side, facing away from me. He looks like he is sleeping. 'These two are dead,' my clerk says. 'That's a negative on your last.' The words are spoken by the radio operator, just like he's talking on the radio. Then he goes 'Huhhh,' real softly and settles into his death. That sets my clerk to shaking violently. He runs back and jumps into the small crater. 'When are we getting out of here?' My words. Before I realize what is happening, I've said it and said it that way. Three octaves too high and panicked. 'Hold on man, hold on,' an arty radio operator yells over to me. His eyes and mine meet. . . . I sink back down in my hole. My chin almost on my knees. A wall of shame and a sudden sweat hit. The final truth. I got nailed. I broke.

"Arty guys are talking. Rounds have been our own arty, they're saying. One gun fired three rounds out of grid before it stopped. 'Here,' yells the arty lieutenant, 'I've got proof.' He walks over to me with a large fragment from a 105mm arty round—one of ours. 'I'll get the bastards for this. I'll get them,' he's ranting."*

"Me"

The first blast blew the canteen from my mouth and knocked me backward and several feet down the embankment. I am on my back, and my eardrums are ringing from the noise. It is the same high-pitched ringing as when I was blown into the trench by a rocket at Khe Sanh. I can't hear very well, but I do hear shouting.

I am trying to come to my senses and get back to a sitting position, but the weight of my gear pins me to the ground. I need to find a hole for cover. I can't sit up using my back muscles, so I roll over onto all fours. From this position I struggle to my feet. I am in shock. My helmet has been blown from my head, my canteen is gone, and I have dirt in my mouth. I make it to my feet and I am covered with

*Ernest Spencer, *Welcome to Vietnam Macho Man: Reflections of a Khe Sanh Vet* (Corps Press, 1987), p 173.

something. The front of my flak jacket, my arms, and my face and hair are covered with what appears to be cottage cheese with red and gray specs. There are larger pieces in my mouth, mixed with the dirt I am spitting onto the ground.

I am momentarily stunned. It is not cottage cheese. It is some Marine's brains. Here comes more fire. We are in the open with no place to hide.

Seeing a smoking crater yards away, I run and jump into it. I feel naked without my combat helmet. A radio operator is dead. Someone is fumbling for the radio, trying to call off the friendly fire. There is brain tissue all over the place. I have had enough.

The medical evacuation helicopter arrives quickly. It didn't have far to fly. We are not that far from major outposts. Bob Awalt had enough. He is down and unconscious from heat stroke. He has no visible wounds. I am nearest to him, so with what strength I have remaining I grab him and maneuver his body into the fireman's carry. Then I pick up his M16 rifle. I don't want to leave his weapon for the enemy. When a soldier goes, his weapon leaves with him. Staggering toward the chopper with Awalt on my back, I see my left arm bleeding. I watch as blood pours down and drips off my elbow into the Vietnamese dirt. I have finally shed some blood for these people. My wound is superficial, but it pours forth a lot more than a few symbolic drops. I am bleeding heavily.

Under the Sea Knight's whirling blades, I find some comfort. They feel like two giant fans. I savor the few seconds it takes to pass under them. I lay Awalt and his M16 on the helicopter ramp. That is as far as I can carry him. He is dragged inside by nameless hands. "He's not dead!" I yell into the open bay of the chopper. I wish I could leave on the chopper, too, but I have ten months remaining in Vietnam. At this moment, America and home never looked or seemed so far away. It is only April. I have found out there is more to this war than West Dickens. The brain residue in my mouth, in my hair, on my face, and all over my flak jacket tells me so.

13: I'm Leaving

1969

It is January 23, 1969. I am leaving Vietnam tomorrow. I have been in Vietnam for more than a year. My flight number is H-20 and my boarding pass number is 71. My service record book (SRB) names nine operations I have been on.

While at Khe Sanh, which was a year ago now, I was on Operation Scotland and Operation Pegasus. When I got that Marine's brains in my mouth, I was on Operation Scotland II. Then I went on Operation Rice, Operation Kentucky, Operation Mameluke Thrust, Operation Allan Brook, and Operation Houston (phase IV). I finally ended my tour participating in Operation Nicollet Bay. I didn't know the names of most operations while I was on them, but I do remember the places. They were all bad.

After being struck by our own artillery near the Cua Viet River, we went to the A Shau Valley, where I witnessed a lot but remember most a Marine on a ridgeline, silhouetted against the rising sun, getting shot by an NVA soldier. I recall that incident at every sunrise I have seen since.

While on an operation in Elephant Valley, northwest of Da Nang, I didn't see any elephants whatsoever, but I managed to find—by stepping on it in a rice paddy—a python nearly twenty feet long.

In Happy Valley, northwest of An Hoa, our column was ambushed by two NVA at a turn in the trail. When I went to put my rifle off safety, it didn't work. A Marine ahead of me fired his M79 grenade launcher at the NVA from close range. The projectile impaled the NVA's head but didn't explode. We had constant trouble in that region. I don't understand why they call such a place "Happy" Valley.

In the area north of An Hoa that the Marines call Dodge City, we stepped off the railroad tracks we were following and took automatic weapons fire from a tree line. While backing up and attempting to take cover, I fell into a deep *punji* pit—a man trap with sharpened bamboo stakes. I fell perfectly between the stakes. Though uninjured, I had to be pulled from the pit by other Marines.

I nearly drowned wading across the river down from the Liberty Bridge.

I dropped my glasses in rice paddy water during an ambush. I found them after about a minute by feeling around in the muddy water, with the Viet Cong taking shots at me all the while. The bullets striking the water around me gave the other Marines, who had already made it to the tree line for cover, cause for a good laugh.

I was ambushed in a graveyard on two occasions. The second time, a Marine free-fired his 60mm mortar at an enemy soldier, who was shooting his automatic weapon at us from the side of the graveyard. The Marine got a direct hit. We all gave him a standing ovation. He took several bows.

I was in skirmishes on special and memorable occasions. I was ambushed on my birthday. I was in a more severe ambush the hour that Senator Robert Kennedy was shot, and yet another the day that Martin Luther King was shot. When that is remembered, I remember I was at Khe Sanh.

We were shot at on so many occasions that I learned to recognize, just by the different sounds and rates of fire, what type of rifle was shooting at us. I was fired at several times by enemy rocket-propelled grenades (RPGs). The noise they make coming through the air always frightened me.

Some soldiers claim they can smell an ambush before it happens. I could never smell one, but I sensed it. When that sense forewarned me that trouble was imminent, the trouble usually started within the minute.

After nearly thirteen months here, I don't rate any medals other than those that my entire regiment earned. But I did get a terrific suntan.

I went on an in-country R and R at China Beach and an out-of-country R and R in Kuala Lumpur, Malaysia. In Kuala Lumpur I heard Beatle songs sung in Chinese. I stayed so drunk for five days that I thought the girl's name I was with was Lee Lee. I didn't know that her real name was Lilly until I got back to Da Nang and looked at a signed picture she gave me of herself.

Homebound

I was awake all last night thinking about going home. Today I see the plane arrive from Okinawa with soldiers just beginning their tour in Vietnam. As I watch them disembark, I realize I am looking at myself thirteen months ago. The soldiers are gathering in formation on the tarmac just as I did.

To these new arrivals, those of us about to leave undoubtedly look like a group of animals that have left a piece of our minds behind forever in Vietnam.

My Magic Carpet Ride

There is wild cheering, hugging, and much shaking of hands. Everybody is in the aisle of the plane. No one is seated or wearing a seat belt. We are going home to America. We survived. Good-bye forever, Vietnam.

Our celebration is brief. Soon all of us are seated, withdrawing into ourselves. We have lots to think about.

I wonder how many body bags are in the luggage compartment of this plane on the way home to relatives and burials in the States. Any one of us up here living could be down there dead. There are a lot of things to think about, and some thoughts are less pleasant than others. I think about my soldier friends—those who are alive and those who aren't.

Okinawa, My Note

I have showered and had a meal. I have been directed to the building where I stored my gear thirteen months earlier on my way to Vietnam. In the building is my seabag, which contains civilian clothes.

Retrieving my seabag, I find at the very top the note I wrote to myself thirteen months earlier, congratulating myself for making it back alive from Vietnam. I laugh as I recall the many times in Vietnam that I was nearly killed. I came close to not making it back here to read this silly note.

The civilian clothes in my bag don't fit anymore because I am much thinner. I have lost weight from living on C rations and patrolling in the jungle's heat.

Tonight we muster at a headquarters near our barracks. Several clerks stand behind a chest-high counter with stacks of papers, which are orders assigning new duty stations for every man who returned on my airplane from Da Nang. As I stand waiting for the paperwork to be processed, I wonder where I will be stationed next. I still have six months left in the Marine Corps.

One clerk finally speaks. "Those of you who enlisted for three or four years active duty in the Marine Corps will find your next duty station written in these orders we're about to hand you."

I hear moans from soldiers who at this moment are regretting having enlisted in the Marines for more than two years. If they had enlisted for only two years, even though they would have been guaranteed being sent to Vietnam, their gamble would have paid off. They have made it back alive.

The clerk continues. "Those of you who enlisted for two years will be discharged within two weeks of your arrival in the United States."

I don't believe it. I am being discharged. It is only January. My two years aren't up until July.

To El Toro

Continental Airlines takes me home from Okinawa. Our plane is fully loaded with returning Marines. Being heavily laden, it seems to use every inch of the long runway during takeoff.

The stewardess passes out paper cups of coffee. I raise the cup to my lips just as we hit severe turbulence. Hot coffee spills everywhere but in my mouth. I am exhausted, so I recline my seat to get some sleep.

My body is on its way home. In my dreams my spirit is trying to find its way home. It seems in a hurry to get there, as if it can't wait for my body in the plane. I dream fitfully into the morning.

America

I watched the sunset as we left Okinawa. Now the sun is coming up and shining through the cabin windows.

Eventually it disappears. The captain says that California is socked in with rainstorms and early-morning fog. He says there is no visibility. I can't see anything from the window of our plane.

El Toro Marine Air Base, Santa Ana, California

One by one, the soldiers descend the steps of the mobile staircase that the ground crew has pushed up to the doorway of the plane. I watch those ahead of me as they alight from the last step onto the tarmac. Each of them pauses a moment and kisses the ground. I will, too. It is good to be home.

Last Days in the Marine Corps

I sign lots of papers. One document is a sworn statement that Vietnam did not affect me in any way whatsoever, that I am okay to go back out and join society.

All week long, recruiters from law enforcement agencies have been talking to us: the California Highway Patrol, the San Diego Police Department, even the motorcycle cops on Catalina Island want us to join. I take their literature and applications and save them, but I want to go home first. I can always be a cop.

I have been given travel pay and a new military identification card. This morning I will be honorably discharged from the U.S. Marine Corps.

I have decided, based on my last flight, not to fly home to New York. I am taking a train. I will ride the Santa Fe's Hiawatha from San Bernardino, California, to Chicago. From Chicago I will catch a bus to New York City. Once I arrive at the city's Port Authority bus terminal, I will take the 8th Avenue subway to the George Washington Bridge bus terminal. From there I will ride the Red and Tan bus line, which crosses the Hudson River on the George Washington Bridge, connects to Route 9W, and heads north into Rockland County. Nyack is only twenty-five miles north of New York City, on the west bank of the Hudson River.

Epilogue

Nyack

It is late evening and I am on the last bus of the day out of New York City. Approaching Nyack from the south along the river road, I estimate I should be at my parents' home in twenty minutes. I will have a short walk.

Only two more stops and I will be off the bus at the bottom of Cedar Hill.

My God, the air is cold. I will carry my seabag up Cedar Hill over my shoulder. Three blocks to go and I am home.

I walk up Cedar Hill Avenue in the dark. It is so cold that my ears ache. I cross Franklin Street and Prospect Street. My parents' home on Mill Street is the next right turn.

In the front yards I walk by, I see stately maple, cedar, and chestnut trees, common to my neighborhood. Leafless now, standing frigid and bare in winter, they are like tall sentinels. They are silent witnesses to my coming home, late on this February night. They are the only witnesses.

The cold cement sidewalk sends a chill through the soles of my black military dress shoes.

Once on Mill Street, I look in the distance toward my home. In the moonlight I see the wavering, uneven cinder block wall in the front yard. I helped my father build that wall when I was ten. I mixed the cement for him in a wheelbarrow.

My parents' home, number 40, is painted white with green shutters; I see the white columns of the front porch.

I am here, standing on the sidewalk. It is late, and the house is dark. My parents and brothers and sisters must all be sleeping.

I stand a moment in the darkness just staring at the house, thinking about the times I thought I would never see home again.

The neighborhood is quiet. All the neighbors must be sleeping, too. Cold February nights are best spent under warm blankets. Tomorrow everyone will rise and go to work and school.

Wisps of smoke from fireplace embers are puffing from the chimneys. No one is awake that I can see; there are no lights in any windows. No one has kept a porch light on. This is the last light that families extinguish before going to bed; until that time, all are welcome at their doors. The street lamp at the corner is on and that is all.

No one is awake to welcome me home because no one knew when I was coming. For Vietnam, we leave alone and return alone.

I sit on the wall I helped my father build, smoke a cigarette, and savor this long-awaited moment at the end of my magic carpet ride.

Inside

Sitting at the dining room table, looking around the room, I see that nothing has changed. We are all gathered: my dad, my mom, my brothers and sisters. Everyone has gotten out of bed.

"Are you all right, Jack?"

"Are you sure you're all right, Jack?"

I hear the question many times.

Whenever I rise from my seat at the table, my family stares at me as if looking to see if I am all here—checking for a limp maybe, looking at my hands and counting fingers.

I repeatedly assure them I am fine. I am. I'm home.

Eventually, my family returns to bed one by one. They all have different schedules tomorrow. Finally my mom and dad retire, too. All say they will see me in the morning.

I am restless now and know that I can't sleep. I will put on some nice civilian clothes and walk downtown. My clothes are at least one size too big because of the weight I lost in Vietnam, but they will have to do. I don't need to wear my Marine uniform any longer. I am a civilian now.

Downtown

Walking downtown, toward the business section in my town, my destination is a bar that isn't closed yet. It is late, but I could use a beer. Suddenly I am back in Nam; I am walking silently and scanning the yards of houses that I pass. I am looking to my right, then left, then back again. I am speed-reading the terrain, looking at the hedge lines, looking for any signs of life or anything out of place. I am looking for Viet Cong and I can't help it.

My hands feel empty. They are grasping for an M16 that isn't there. I feel naked without my weapon. I feel helpless. Carrying my weapon for a year made it part of me; without it I feel vulnerable, like easy prey.

I haven't come home alone after all. I have brought Vietnam with me.

O'Donoghue's Tavern

The bar is open. I will go inside and see if I can find a familiar face. The heat inside is a welcome relief from the frigid air outdoors on this cold February night; I should have put on warmer clothes before I walked here.

There is a vacant stool at the center of the bar. Seated, I remember a year and a half in the past. It was the afternoon that Dunnigan walked into this bar. The following morning I enlisted in the Marines. It seems like a century ago. I remember Dunnigan's shrapnel wound to his head, which he suffered in Vietnam. Now I know, having been to Vietnam, that he wouldn't have received that wound if he had kept his helmet on. It would have stopped the shrapnel.

All the patrons have long hair. The owner, whom I know, is bartending. He quickly places a beer in front of me and says it is on the house. I thank him, then turn and look around. Patrons are talking about a place called Woodstock. Some are making plans to go during the upcoming summer. The bar television is on with the late-night news. I haven't watched a television show in a year and a half.

The newscast is showing the latest film footage from Vietnam. The segment shows soldiers firing into a tree line. The soundman with the photographer made sure that the noise of automatic weapons fire was recorded very loud and very clear for special effects. The footage looks staged to me.

My war isn't over yet. I can watch my war on television in the bars.

People in the bar are happy. They are joking, smiling, laughing, and having a good time. I am trying to smile along with them, but I can't. Nothing is funny anymore. Vietnam changed me into a serious person and robbed me of my youth. Vietnam made me an old man. I no longer feel comfortable with my peers.

All the patrons have skin tones that are sickly shades of winter white. They will have to wait until summer for their suntans. My skin is bronze. I am deeply tanned from a year of crossing open fields and rice paddies under Vietnam's tropical sun, all the while fighting off heat stroke and the Viet Cong.

The newscast continues. Following the story on the Vietnam War, another story is broadcast with more footage about a college campus demonstration. It shows students carrying signs and banners protesting America's involvement in the war, the war that I just left and, thankfully, survived.

The television cameraman focuses on several signs; one reads, "Stop the killing." Another protest sign carried by a student reads, "Make love not war." A sign that reads "Baby killers" bothers me. I recall the little Vietnamese children in the villages and along the roadsides to whom many of us gave our last C rations while we did without.

I think how wrong that sign is. If the demonstrators only knew. I remember the Vietnamese kid behind the wall, the one who taunted us right after we were ambushed down in the Badlands—the Arizona territory of Vietnam. I remember that long, long day of firefights and pulling down a Marine's arm that held his loaded .45 pistol, to give the kid a chance to get away.

I remember my foxhole, West Dickens; the exploding ammo dump; the sniper bullet through my hair; being blown into a trench line by a rocket; Lang Vei; the Bravo patrol that never made it back; waiting to be overrun by NVA, who outnumbered us seven to one; being shelled, rocketed, and mortared night and day; the *punji* pit; and floundering in a rice paddy under fire while searching for my glasses. I remember much, much more, and I still shudder and spit when I recall that Marine's brains blown into my mouth.

I have seen both sides, not just the two scenes on this television news. I have been there.

Sharon

Ah! Someone in this bar recognizes me, and she is approaching. It is Sharon. It's Sharon! I had a crush on her in school.

She stares at me, giving me a long, inquisitive look. Maybe she will join me for a drink. Maybe I will get lucky on my first night home.

"Jack? Jack? Is that you, Jack? You have such a beautiful, dark suntan. Where did you get it? Where have you been, on vacation in Florida?"

Florida? I can't answer her. I am truly at a loss for words.